101

Games That Teach
Storytelling Skills

Anthony Burcher
Michelle "Mike" Burcher

D1294846

HEALTHY
LEARNING™

ISBN: 978-1-60679-231-5
Library of Congress Control Number: 2012942568
Cover design: Studio J Art & Design
Book layout: Studio J Art & Design
Front cover photo: iStockphoto/Thinkstock

Healthy Learning
P.O. Box 1828
Monterey, CA 93942
www.healthylearning.com

Dedication

In memory of Ray and Wendy, whose absence
continually reminds us of the importance of story.

Acknowledgments

The authors thank all those who have unwittingly found their way into our stories, including but not limited to: Allene Gywnn, Henry Brown, Ray and Dorothy Burcher, Jeanne Wilson Booker, friends from Camp Albemarle and Makemie Woods, and Bucky the Cat. We appreciate those people whose stories and games continue to inspire us, especially Donald Davis, and also the Weavers of the Word, the TellTale Hearts Storytelling Theatre, VASA, and the family of the Annual Recreation Workshop. Mostly, we thank our God, whose story is timeless and life-changing and the reason we tell stories at all.

Foreword

Storytelling is more deeply important than simply entertainment. *101 Games That Teach Storytelling Skills* introduces the historic depth of this ancient art form and its present importance in each of our families and each of our working lives. This resource reminds us that storytelling is not casually trivial, but deeply meaningful and important.

Through this book, the Burchers lead us into experiencing and learning about storytelling through play!

The exercises and storytelling games take a large and complicated "meal" and break it down into small, digestible, and enjoyable "bites" that can be joyfully taken in by people of all ages.

This book is a remarkable combination of important work accomplished through delightful play. What could be better?

You will love diving into *101 Games That Teach Storytelling Skills*, and you will find yourself returning to it as a practical and useful resource again and again.

—Donald Davis

Tom Raymond

Contents

   #1: Astounding Adjective Name Game

   #2: Adjective Versus Adverb

   #3: By Just Looking at Me

   #4: Most Interesting Place These Shoes Have Been

   #5: Did You Take the Cookie?

   #6: Take Only What You Need

   #7: Story Starter Marathon

   #8: "I Have Never ..." Chair Swap—Story Prompts

   #9: Observation Challenge

   #10: Pick Three

   #11: The Doctor's Dog

   #12: Who's Missing?

   #13: Roll and Remember

   #14: Soccer Ball Story Ball

   #15: Just Like

   #16: Dear Advice Lady

   #17: E Is Overused

   #18: Spell Trap

   #19: Word Association Challenge

   #20: Word Convergence

   #21: Proverb Remix

Chapter 3: Games That Primarily Teach the Skills Needed to Tell Stories in Front of an Audience

Preface

The Value of Storytelling

Throughout history, and especially before history, stories have been passed from generation to generation, giving the listeners a sense of identity and purpose. Stories entertained, taught valuable lessons, and preserved the common experience. Using gesture and facial expression, descriptive words, dance, and song, storytellers painted pictures on the canvas of the mind.

Before the advent of written language, storytellers carefully remembered and told again and again the heroics and foibles of their ancestors, as they had learned the stories from storytellers before them. The role of the storyteller in the community was one of historian, entertainer, teacher, and motivational speaker. More interested in communicating a sense of truth rather than factual accuracy, the oldest known stories are steeped in vivid, fanciful, and exaggerated details that stir the imagination and invite the listeners to participate in the story. Because of the truth they communicate, similar themes are found among the various and diverse cultures of the world. As purveyors of these truths, the storyteller had great influence and responsibility.

One of the most well-known and effective storytellers was Jesus of Nazareth. Through parables, Jesus used everyday, common experiences to communicate layers of truth to the listeners. Hearing Jesus speak, they could see in their minds the farmer planting and harvesting, or the house built on sand being washed out to sea. They could imagine a king's banquet table; they understood the traditions of women waiting with lamps at a wedding. In these stories, the listeners not only heard the message, but they identified themselves as part of the story. These parables were so effective and influential that Jesus was persecuted by the religious leaders for telling these stories.

There are many definitions of storytelling. The National Council of Teachers of English defines storytelling as "relating a tale to one or more listeners through voice and gesture." Others include dance, song, or visual media as storytelling. All definitions acknowledge that storytelling involves three components: a teller, a listener, and the story being told. All three interact. The success of the story, whether entertainment or educational, depends on the teller engaging the listener, and the listener's willingness to enter into the story.

In the past century, the development of recorded sound, cinema, and digital media has greatly changed how many in our culture tell stories. Whether visual images, digital graphics, and special effects enhance or detract from the audience's ability to imagine can be debated. The reality is that good storytelling draws the listener into the compelling story.

Storytelling is at the heart of effective communication. Whether recounting cultural history, testifying to an inspiring, life-changing experience, teaching a valuable lesson, marketing a product, or simply entertaining, the essential elements of good storytelling communicate the message. Facial expression and body language, descriptive words, and clear presentation all contribute to communication. Consider the difference between someone simply saying the word "hot," versus someone saying the word with a pained expression, their hand recoiled. The body language conveys that something touched was very hot, yet the word spoken is the same. Or consider these two phrases: "There was a house on hill," versus "There was dark and gloomy house perched on the jagged cliff." The second inspires a much clearer picture of what the teller intends to convey to the listener, improving the communication.

The games in *101 Games That Teach Storytelling Skills* teach and reinforce these important communication skills and inspire confidence. These games can be played just for fun, or used to reinforce a particular skill. Whether the leader is a professional storyteller, a teacher, a historian, a preacher, or a camp counselor, the participants will enjoy laughing and learning together.

The Critical Need for Storytelling

The technology of the 21st century has brought many benefits, and it has come with a cost. A growing dependence on electronic communication has limited opportunities to learn and practice essential communication skills. E-mail, texting, and social networking sites have taken over personal communication, reducing language to incomplete sentences, incomplete words, and clichés. Even the advance of video filmmaking, allowing the performers to have their presentation edited and enhanced with special effects, has greatly affected public performance. The art of live performance, in which an individual or cast reacts and interacts with the emotions of the audience, is quickly being lost.

Today's children and youth have fewer opportunities to develop the much-needed skills for interpersonal, face-to-face communication, let alone live performance. These technologies have made the younger generations more intimidated by the prospect of speaking in front of others, or even of simply having a personal conversation. Many kids choose to text someone sitting in the same room instead of speaking to them. Many youth post personal information and secrets on the Internet that they would never say to someone face-to-face. As a result, they rarely learn to gauge how someone reacts to what they have said, and they themselves do not learn how to listen and respond appropriately.

Storytelling and Camps

The camp setting is ideal for teaching these essential communication skills. Away from the cell phones and computers, campers and staff alike practice communicating on a personal level, in an environment that is supportive and encouraging. Campers are encouraged to tell about high and low points of each day, so they have opportunities to reflect on their life experience, and they learn to listen to the personal stories of others. Simple skills like listening without interrupting and speaking using descriptive words are practiced and enhanced.

Storytelling has long been a part of the camp culture and experience. Stories around the campfire, bedtime tales, devotional reflections, and stories about the wilderness experience itself are an important aspect of camp programming. Many campers say that these opportunities to tell and listen to stories, getting to know new people on a deeper level, and building face-to-face, honest relationships are the highlight of their camp experience.

Our obligation as camp and educational professionals is to create a safe environment for learning. Because most camps very intentionally have limited technology, this makes camp an ideal setting for learning these social and linguistic skills. When this practice is fun and creative, it stimulates the imagination and breaks down barriers. The games in this book are intended to provide opportunities for free expression, laughter, and discovery of the storyteller in all of us.

Introduction

How to Use This Resource to Teach the Skills of Storytelling

This book is divided into three groups of games:

- Games that primarily teach the skills you need before you step in front of an audience (Chapter 2)
- Games that primarily teach the skills you need in front of an audience (Chapter 3)
- Games where participants are actually telling a story in front of and with each other (Chapter 4)

Before the description of each game, the leader/teacher will find the essentials of that game. This makes selecting the correct game for your purposes much faster. The essesntials include the following:

- *Game Objective:* Helps the leader select games that match the interests of the group. An example of a game objective in a tag game would be "avoid being tagged."
- *Learning Goal:* See if this game will help with the skills you wish your group to practice.
- *Recommended Ages:* Some games work with better with adults; others are more appropriate for a younger group. This will help you match games that work best for your participants
- *Number of Players:* A quick reference to help the leader in planning. However, we all know that sometimes three people sign up for your workshop and 30 show up, or vice-versa.
- *Energy Level:* Varying the energy level can help keep your group engaged. Bouncing back and forth between high and low energy levels is not recommended.
- *Formation:* Plan what works for your space. Not every game will safely fit in every play area, classroom, or workshop space.
- *Props:* As a final bit of preparation, you need to know what props you should gather. This book uses very few props, but does occasionally call for a few inexpensive, easy-to-find items: a pair of dice, some playing cards, a tin can, and such.

The authors have each been recreation leaders for well over 25 years. Congratulations to you, the reader/user of this book. If you haven't been already, you are now a recreation leader as well. Following are a few of recreation leadership's finer points:

- *Know your group.* If any game here or anywhere might bring out immature behavior that could lead to inappropriate words or touch, don't play that game.
- *Be safe.* Keep your play area clear of any obstructions, sharp objects, fragile items, and the like.
- *Plan ahead.* Use the tools given in this book to create a safe, challenging learning environment for your lesson or workshop. However, don't be afraid to change your plan if something is not working.
- *"Do" your instructions.* Don't tell your group the sound or motion they are going to make. Show them, and then have them do it. Now, they are more likely to be invested in the game and will pay better attention to its rules.
- *Have fun, and your participants will have fun, too.* Storytelling is fun. Recreation is fun. There is no reason using recreation to teach storytelling shouldn't be fun as well.

Teach well, play well, tell well, and have fun!

1

The Essential Skills
for Storytelling

Photodisc

Anyone seeking to teach others to become better storytellers needs to learn and focus on the particular skills of the art form. A good storyteller will always be practicing and honing these skills. The goal of *101 Games That Teach Storytelling Skills* is to make that practice fun. For a list of the games that can be used to practice each of the following skills, refer to Appendix A: Games That Best Teach the Essential Skills.

The 10 Skills Needed to Perform in Front of an Audience

- *Facial Expressions:* Does the storyteller's face enhance the emotions of the story?

- *Gestures:* Does the storyteller's body language support what the storyteller's mouth is saying?

- *Eye Contact:* Does the storyteller (venue permitting) attempt to look in every audience member's eyes at least once per story?

- *Reading the Audience and Negotiating With the Audience:* Does the storyteller react to what the audience is saying? Is the teller paying attention to the audience's body language, laughs, gasps, and other cues, and then adapt to improve the listeners' experience?

- *Descriptive Ability:* Does the teller provide enough of a visual painting?

- *Tempo:* Do the storyteller's words come out too fast or too slow for the story being told and the type of audience present?

- *Voice Inflection:* Do all the vocal ranges used support the story and its characters and their emotions?

- *Diction:* Does the storyteller speak clearly?

- *Projection:* Can the storyteller be heard by everyone in the audience?

- *Enthusiasm:* Is the most excited person for the story the storyteller?

The 10 Skills Needed *Before* Performing in Front of an Audience

- *Imagination:* Everyone has it, but using it well is a skill that needs to be practiced.

- *Discovering Personal Stories:* Some people never tell personal stories, some tell only personal stories, and some tell both. This book includes games that can help you or your class work on finding those hidden personal stories.

- *Discovering Stories to Make Your Own:* This skill is old-fashioned *research*. Sadly, no games can replace the essential hard work of finding and citing sources. However, this book can help the telling of those wonderful fairytales, fables, or Jack Tales, which become the storyteller's unique presentation.

- *Sensory Addition:* When practicing a story, the teller should constantly ask himself, "Where in this story can I include one or more of the five senses?"

- *Word Selection:* Part of a quality practice session is asking, "Am I using the best words possible to describe my scenes, characters, actions, and such?" Don't aim for the biggest words; aim for the best words. A storyteller is not a thesaurus, but needs to have a solid understanding of the language he is using and the selection of words available. Several games in this book explore the huge variety of words and phrases in the English language including puns, palindromes, hinky-pinkys, spoonerisms, and so forth.

- *Powers of Observation:* An effective storyteller is a people-watcher. Storytellers need to be experts on how people, sound, act, react, move, smell, and think. We cannot "report" the world if we do not see and know the world.

- *Creation and Creativity:* Imagination and creativity are different things. It is not enough to simply have an imagination; nearly everyone on the planet does. It is the gifted storyteller who takes what is in his imagination or memory and turns it into a story that others want to hear.

- *Dedication to Practice:* Whether working alone, in tandem, or in a troupe, the storyteller needs to practice. This skill is one of the most important. It is hard, necessary work. You hold in your hand 101 ways to make that work fun.

- *An Above-Average Understanding and Command of the English Language (or the Language in Which You Are Telling):* Some of your characters will speak with excellent grammar, some of your characters will speak with poor grammar, and the storyteller needs to know the difference. As tellers, we sometimes break the rules of our language to make the story more pleasing to the ear, but we still need to know the rules and understand them. Example: Audiences like to hear, "Jack wondered what the egg was made of." Most audiences do not care for the more proper, "Jack wondered of what the egg was made."

- *An Above-Average Understanding of What Constitutes a "Story":* Not all "happenings" are stories. The three vital elements of a story are *place, character(s),* and *conflict.* There is no story without these three elements.

Games That Primarily Teach the Skills Needed *Before* Telling a Story in Front of an Audience

Wavebreak Media/Thinkstock

#1: Astounding Adjective Name Game

Game Objective: To learn the names of the other participants
Learning Objective: To practice the skills of word selection and mastery of language
Recommended Ages: 10 to 110
Number of Players: 2 to 30
Energy Level: Low
Formation: Sitting in chairs in a circle
Props: None

Description:

- Encourage each player to think of an adjective that both describes himself *and* begins with the same letter or sound as his first name.
- Allow about 30 seconds for everyone to think of an appropriate adjective.
- Tell your group that each person, in turn, will introduce himself using his adjective; however, before each player introduces himself, he will try to name all the people who went before him.
- Begin the game by introducing yourself to the group, and allow play to move around the circle.
- Example:
    Leader: I am Amazing Anthony
    Teller #1: Amazing Anthony, and I am Merry Mike.
    Teller #2: Amazing Anthony, Merry Mike, and I am Silly Sarah.
    Teller #3: Amazing Anthony, Merry Mike, Silly Sarah, and I am Jolly Joshua.

Leadership Tips:

- As leader, conclude the game by naming everyone in the circle.
- If the group is large, shorten the game by having each person name only the three people closest to him.
- Every good recreation or workshop leader has a handful of tried-and-true name games in his pocket, and this one works well.

#2: Adjective Versus Adverb

Game Objective: To be the first player to yell out an adjective or adverb

Learning Objective: To improve the skills of word selection and command of the English language

Recommended Ages: 12 to 112

Number of Players: 2 to 100

Energy Level: Medium

Formation: Standing and facing each other in pairs

Props: None

Description:

- Review adjectives and adverbs with your group. An adjective modifies or describes a noun, and an adverb modifies the meaning of a verb, another adverb, or an adjective. (Adverbs usually, generally, mostly end in *-ly*.)
- Instruct your group to find and face a partner.
- Tell each player to place one hand behind his back.
- At the count of three, each player will show his partner either a thumbs-up or a thumbs-down.
- Explain that if the thumbs match (either thumbs-up or thumbs-down), each player wants to be the first of his pair to yell out an adjective.
- If the thumbs do not match, each player wants to be the first of his pair to yell out an adverb.
- Loudly and enthusiastically count to three, and watch the fun.
- Before playing a second round, instruct players to use any adjective or adverb only once, making the game more challenging and helpful.
- After two or three rounds with the same partner, invite your participants to find a new partner and begin again.

Leadership Tip:

- As leader, be aware that your group could have an odd number of people, and you may need to play.

#3: By Just Looking at Me

Game Objective: To help participants learn more about each other

Learning Objective: To search for hidden stories in how you believe others perceive you

Recommended Ages: 10 to 100

Number of Players: 2 to 30

Energy Level: Low

Formation: Sitting in chairs in a circle

Props: None

Description:

- Begin this game by saying out loud the partial phrase, "You wouldn't think by just looking at me, but I ..."
- Offer some information about yourself that most folks do not know about you or would not think you do. Examples:
  - ✓ I raise chickens.
  - ✓ I like to knit.
  - ✓ I used to be a cheerleader.
  - ✓ I am an award-winning chef.
- Go around the circle, and have each person, in turn, say and complete the phrase with something interesting about himself.

Leadership Tip:

- As leader, be prepared to gently dig a little deeper in the information you hear to discover any hidden personal stories.

#4: Most Interesting Place These Shoes Have Been

Game Objective: To learn about the other people in a group

Learning Objective: To improve the skill of discovering your own stories

Recommended Ages: 10 to 100

Number of Players: 2 to 30

Energy Level: Low

Formation: Sitting in chairs in a circle

Props: Everyone in your group should have on some sort of footwear.

Description:

- Invite everyone in the group to lean back in their chairs, stick their feet out in front of themselves, and stare at their shoes.
- Ask everyone to think about the most interesting place those shoes have been.
- Taking turns around the circle, encourage participants to tell about the most interesting place those shoes have been.
- Conclude by asking participants to think of all the clothes they have at home and all the stories those clothes could tell.

Leadership Tips:

- This game is a great "get to know you" exercise.
- Be prepared to hear a lot of stories people may have never considered were stories.
- Almost always there is someone in the group who just bought his shoes yesterday. Ask that person where in the world they would most like to go in those shoes.

#5: Did You Take the Cookie?

Game Objective: To create an alibi with players' initials
Learning Objective: To work with the skills of imagination and word selection
Recommended Ages: 14 to 114
Number of Players: 2 to 25
Energy Level: Low
Formation: Sitting in chairs in a circle
Props: None

Description:

- Go around the circle, and ask each person to share his name and initials.
- Tell everyone that you are going to go around the circle and ask each person, in turn, the accusatory question: "Did you take the cookie?"
- Explain that each participant will offer a short alibi based on his initials. Share some examples, such as "Jack Levi Turner might answer "Just left town," Anthony Wayne Burcher could answer, "Always watching baseball," or Michelle Anne Dickerson might reply, "My appointment delayed."
- After everyone understands the examples and instructions, turn to the player on your right or left and ask, "Did you take the cookie?"
- Allow the game to move around the circle until everyone has shared an alibi, essentially a complete, creative story in three words.

Leadership Tip:

- Be mindful that some folks have four, two, and occasionally just one initial.

#6: Take Only What You Need

Game Objective: To get to know other participants

Learning Objective: To search for hidden personal stories

Recommended Ages: 12 to 112

Number of Players: 2 to 25

Energy Level: Low

Formation: Sitting in chairs in a circle

Props: A roll of toilet tissue with clearly defined, perforated squares

Description:

- Before the game begins, have in your mind two examples of a time from your past when you got in trouble. Naturally, these should be stories you are willing to share openly.
- Stand in front of the group, hold up the roll of toilet tissue, and tear off two squares.
- Hand the roll to the person sitting on your right, and give only these simple instructions: "Take only what you need."
- Instruct the group to keep taking and passing the toilet tissue until everyone has at least one square. (Be prepared for some people to take one square and some to take seven or eight.)
- Once everyone has their toilet tissue, explain these are "Trouble Squares" and each person will tell about different times they got into trouble, one tale for each square they took.
- As leader, you will want to lead by example and begin the sharing session with your two tales.
- From this point forward, simply move around the circle letting people briefly tell of times they got in trouble.
- After everyone has told, ask the group which tales they heard they would like to know more about and which tales the teller should consider putting together as a full story.

Leadership Tips:

- Do not play this game if you are short on time.
- For the environmentally conscious in the group, suggest everyone pocket their clean tissues and use them later for cleaning up spills, runny noses, children's faces, eye glasses, and the like.

#7: Story Starter Marathon

Game Objective: To win the race

Learning Objective: To develop the skill of discovering personal stories

Recommended Ages: 7 to 107

Number of Players: 2 to 20

Energy Level: Medium to high (depending on the group)

Formation: Group will stand at a well-defined starting line facing a well-marked finish line (Consider the size of your play area and the age and energy level of your group to decide how far apart these lines should be.)

Props: Any easily seen line markers such as cones, rope, tape, or chairs

Description:

- Before the race, you will need to write down or mentally prepare a list of story prompts (ideas that spark forgotten stories).
- With your group lined up on the starting line, let them know that you will call out a story prompt and a movement direction.
- If the group members fall into the specific category of the story prompt, they will follow the movement direction that sends them ideally closer to the finish line.
- Following are a dozen examples to get you started:
  - ✓ If you have ever lost your keys, take four baby steps forward.
  - ✓ If you have ever gotten lost in a bad neighborhood, take one giant step forward.
  - ✓ If you were ever sent to the principal's office, take three hops forward.
  - ✓ If you have ever stolen a watermelon, take two skips forward.
  - ✓ If you have ever received kindness when you didn't deserve it, take one giant leap forward.
  - ✓ If you have ever overcooked or undercooked something, take two jumps forward.
  - ✓ If you have ever had an item of clothing fall off in public, take one step backward.
  - ✓ If you have ever gotten a parking ticket, take three hops on one leg forward.
  - ✓ If you have ever been asked to leave somewhere, take two baby steps backward.
  - ✓ If you have ever met someone important, but you did not know until later, take one hop forward.
  - ✓ If you have ever eaten something you wish you hadn't, take one hop backward.
  - ✓ If you have ever gone to the bathroom, not in a bathroom, take one adult step forward.

Design Pics/Thinkstock

- Congratulate the first player who crosses the finish line.
- Sit your group down to conclude this event with a discussion about which prompt(s) they heard made them recall a potentially forgotten story.

Leadership Tips:

- Always make sure your play space is free of any obstructions.
- You can control the tempo of this game by using both forward and backward commands.
- This race works well in a small space (such as a room) or a large space (such as a field). In a small space, use commands such as "baby steps" and "hop once." In a large space use commands such as "leaps," "giant steps," and "skips."
- If your group is active, nimble, young, or young at heart, use lots of movement.

#8: "I Have Never ..." Chair Swap—Story Prompts

Game Objective: To not be the one player left standing without a chair

Learning Objective: To discover hidden personal stories

Recommended Ages: 10 to 110

Number of Players: 6 to 50

Energy Level: High

Formation: Sitting in chairs in a circle with no chair for the leader, who stands in the center

Props: A chair for every person, minus one

Description:

- Tell your group that you are going to make an "I have never ..." statement such as, "I have never been surfing" or "I have never been on a horse."
- When you make this statement, explain that anyone who has done what you have never done must get up and run to a new chair while you try to claim an empty chair for yourself. Make sure your group understands that the person left standing in the center will be the next person to call out an "I have never ..." statement.
- Allow this active game to continue until just before the group begins to get tired of it.
- Conclude this activity by asking the group if they have done something they had forgotten about until playing this game.

Leadership Tip:

- This game reminds people of things they have done but forgotten and can be an excellent place to discover lost stories.

#9: Observation Challenge

Game Objective: To identify three things that have changed about your partner
Learning Objective: To practice the skill of observation
Recommended Ages: 8 to 108
Number of Players: 2 to 100
Energy Level: Low
Formation: People in pairs, facing each other—either standing or sitting
Props: Only what participants are wearing or have with them

Description:

- Place your group in pairs, and instruct them to spend the next 10 seconds studying their partner.
- Ask participants to turn back-to-back and then alter three things about their appearance. You might suggest buttoning or unbuttoning something, moving rings, bracelets, or watches, tying or untying something, and such.
- After about 30 seconds, invite participants to turn face-to-face and try to identify the three visual changes their partner made.
- After about one minute, encourage people to give their partner hints if he has not yet guessed all three changes.

Leadership Tips:

- This game does not have to be a race to identify the three changes, but it can be if your group would benefit and enjoy it.
- This can be a "get to know each other" game, by having the pairs talk about a favorite pet or sibling while observing the other person.

#10: Pick Three

Game Objective: To discover what a small group has in common
Learning Objective: To practice the skill of observation
Recommended Ages: 10 to 110
Number of Players: 8 to 30
Energy Level: Low
Formation: Sitting in chairs in a circle
Props: None

Description:

- Begin the game by asking three people in your group to stand. What your group does not know is that you chose these three because they have something in common (examples: all wearing watches, all have pierced ears, all have glasses, all wearing jeans, etc.).
- Invite your group to guess what you saw the three people having in common.
- If more rounds are desired, ask the person who guessed correctly to pick three more people with something in common to stand.

Leadership Tip:

- Sometimes, you may need to remind the group that many people have many things in common. It is not enough to say they all have skin, hair, or clothing, or that they are playing this game. The group needs to guess what *you observed* the three had in common.

iStockphoto/Thinkstock

#11: The Doctor's Dog

Game Objective: To keep a constantly changing chant moving around the circle
Learning Objective: To work on word selection and vocabulary development skills
Recommended Ages: 10 to 110
Number of Players: 2 to 30
Energy Level: Medium
Formation: Sitting in chairs in a circle
Props: None

Description:

- Have your group repeat after you: "The doctor's dog is a dainty dog."
- Have your group repeat after you a second time, except this time participants slap their knees on "doctor" and "dainty" and clap their hands each time the word "dog" is spoken.
- Practice several times until the group has the chant totally mastered.
- On the last practice round, have each person, in turn, say the chant while the group continues the knees and hand clapping. The chant should begin and end with the leader.
- Explain to the group that things are now going to get tougher. On their turn speaking, they are going to have to substitute the word "dainty" with another adjective that begins with the letter D.
- The test is to see if the group can send the chant all the way around the circle without missing the beat or missing a word.
- If you desire a second round, have a participant suggest a different profession and build a new chant off that, such as "The mechanic's macaw is a mellow macaw," "The lawyer's lion is a lazy lion," or "The preacher's platypus is a playful platypus."
- Example:
    Leader: The doctor's dog is a dainty dog.
    Player #1: The doctor's dog is a dirty dog.
    Player #2: The doctor's dog is a despicable dog.
    Player #3: The doctor's dog is a delightful dog.
    Player #4: The doctor's dog is a dangerous dog.
    Leader: The doctor's dog is a dramatic dog. Good job, group. Who would like to suggest a new profession?

#12: Who's Missing?

Game Objective: To discover the missing player
Learning Objective: To enhance powers of observation
Recommended Ages: 6 to 106
Number of Players: 8 to 30
Energy Level: Medium
Formation: Standing in a circle
Props: None

Description:

- With participants standing in a circle, instruct them to close their eyes.
- Explain to your group that they are all going to find a new place in the circle with their eyes closed, while the "secret person" (the person you tap) will open his eyes and depart the room. Secretly tap one player on the shoulder.
- Encourage the group to move slowly and put their hands up as "bumpers" so that all are safe.
- Once everyone has reformed as a circle, or something close, invite players to open their eyes, raise their hands, and make guesses as to who the missing person is.
- If a second round is desired, allow the person who guessed correctly to choose the next secret person.

Leadership Tips:

- Make sure your play area is free of all obstructions.
- This game works best if the group has had time to get to know each other.

#13: Roll and Remember

Game Objective: To discover stories at the roll of a die

Learning Objective: To uncover forgotten stories with your senses

Recommended Ages: 10 to 110

Number of Players: 2 to 30

Energy Level: Low

Formation: Sitting in chairs in a circle

Props: One die, and one sheet of paper with the following numbered words written in large letters:

- #1 = Smelled
- #2 = Seen
- #3 = Heard
- #4 = Tasted
- #5 = Touched
- #6 = Stepped in

Description:

- Before the game, set the paper on the floor, in the center of the circle so all can see it.
- Hand the die to the player on your right, and ask him to roll the die on the piece of paper.
- If the player rolls a one, he has to tell of the worst thing he ever smelled.
- Each player, in turn, moving around the circle, will tell the worst thing he experienced using the sheet of paper as a guide.
- If you wish to play a second round, ask players to tell of the best thing they have ever smelled, seen, heard, or such.

Leadership Tips:

- Let the players define the words as they wish. For example, "heard" could be the worst thing spoken to them or the most obnoxious noise they ever heard.
- As the leader, play or don't play, depending on your time.

#14: Soccer Ball Story Ball

Game Objective: To catch a ball and test your memory
Learning Objective: To find forgotten personal stories
Recommended Ages: 10 to 110
Number of Players: 3 to 30
Energy Level: Medium
Formation: Sitting in a circle
Props: A permanent marker and a toy soccer ball, preferably stuffed, but an actual soccer ball will work as well

Description:

- Explain to your group that a standard soccer ball has 32 spaces made of either hexagons or pentagons, and in each of these spaces you have written 32 places.
- Begin the game by gently tossing the ball to any player in the circle and asking that person to catch the ball and look under his right thumb and state out loud the "place" found below.
- Now ask the person holding the ball if he ever got into trouble in that place. If so, ask him to share that story. If not, ask him to carefully pass the ball to someone else in the circle.
- Continue to play until everyone has had a chance to catch the ball.

Leadership Tip:

- 75% of the time or higher, someone will have a "lost" story about that place. The following 32 places can be written on your soccer ball story ball:

✓ Living room	✓ Locker room	✓ Vacation
✓ Bathroom	✓ Restroom	✓ Grandparent's
✓ Bedroom	✓ School play	house
✓ Garage	✓ Library	✓ Friend's house
✓ Basement	✓ Recess	✓ Ball field
✓ Attic	✓ Gym class	✓ Car
✓ Kitchen	✓ School bus	✓ Place of worship
✓ Principal's office	✓ School cafeteria	✓ Playground
✓ Science class	✓ Math class	✓ Backyard
✓ Art class	✓ Parking lot	✓ Relative's house
✓ Music class	✓ Grocery store	✓ Summer camp

#15: Just Like

Game Objective: To have everyone in the group connect creatively
Learning Objective: To practice the skill of imagination and creativity
Recommended Ages: 8 to 108
Number of Players: 3 to 30
Energy Level: Low
Formation: Sitting in chairs in a circle
Props: None

Description:

- Going to the right, ask each person in the group to share one present they would like to receive on their next birthday.
- Pay attention to the answer of the person directly on your left, and finish this round by sharing your answer.
- Begin the second round by sharing how what you want is "just like" what the person just before you wanted. (Example: "My puppy is just like your puzzle because they both make a mess on the floor.")
- Tell the group to follow your example, and explain how the present they wish is "just like" what the person sitting on their left wanted.
- Continue around the circle until everyone has had a turn, and finish by complimenting your group on the nice job they did stretching their imaginations.
- Three-player example round:
    Leader: I want a car for my next birthday.
    Teller #1: I want a guitar.
    Teller #2: I want a new dress.
    Teller #3: I want a new television.
    Leader: Well, my car is just like your television because they are both high-tech.
    Teller #1: Well, my guitar is just like your car because I can make it roar.
    Teller #2: And my new dress is just like your guitar because we have the same shape.
    Teller #3: My television is just like your new dress because it is only good when it is on.

Leadership Tip:

- If a teller is having trouble making a "just like" connection, encourage others in the group to suggest connections, then let the teller choose the one he thinks fits best and complete the sentence.

#16: Dear Advice Lady

Game Objective: To reimagine a character's plight and share a plea for help

Learning Objective: To work with skills of imagination, creativity, and understanding of what comprises a story

Recommended Ages: 14 to 114

Number of Players: 2 to 12

Energy Level: Low

Formation: Sitting in chairs in a circle

Props: Pen/pencil and paper for each participant

Description:

- Lead your group in choosing a familiar story from fairy tales, tall tales, literature, the bible, history, or the like.
- From that chosen story, select a main character from the tale.
- Instruct your group to write a letter as that character to the local newspaper's "Dear Advice Lady," asking for help in whatever situation they always find themselves.
- Allow the group about five minutes to write their letter, and finish by having each read his letter out loud to the group. Following is an example letter for Snow White from *Snow White and the Seven Dwarfs*:

> Dear Advice Lady,
>
> I have recently found myself in several awkward, tiring situations. I am now living with seven men. They are nice, tiny men, but I love another. Also, unexpectedly, I have developed a craving for fresh fruit. Please help.
>
> Ready for a Nap,
> Snow White

Leadership Tip:

- You may wish to play a second round in which Dear Advice Lady writes a reply.

#17: E Is Overused

Game Objective: To answer a question without using a word that contains the letter E

Learning Objective: To improve vocabulary, word selection, and command of the English language

Recommended Ages: 10 to 110

Number of Players: 2 to 30

Energy Level: Low

Formation: Sitting in chairs in a circle

Props: None

Description:

- Turn to the player on your right, and ask a simple, common knowledge question, and just before he answers, let the group know that the letter "E" is overused. On their turns, participants must try to answer without using a word that contains the letter "E."
- After the player on your right answers as best he can, let him know that he can now ask the person on his right a question.
- Allow this game to continue around the circle until you are the last to answer a question.

    Leader: What day comes after Monday?

    Player #1: A day similar to today. (Asking next player) What planet do you live on?

    Player #2: Mars' pal. (Asking next player) What month is Christmas?

    Player #3: Our last month. (Asking next player) What do hens lay? (How would you answer?)

Leadership Tip:

- Encourage your group to keep the questions simple.

#18: Spell Trap

Game Objective: To not be the player to finish spelling a word

Learning Objective: To improve the skills of word selection and command of the English language

Recommended Ages: 12 to 112

Number of Players: 2 to 12

Energy Level: Low

Formation: Sitting in chairs in a circle

Props: None

Description:

- Inform your participants that the group is going to spell a word one letter per person at a time, and in this game they don't want to be the person to add the last letter.
- Describe how you are going to start with one letter, and the person sitting next to you will offer a letter, and so forth around the circle.
- Explain the two main "No-no's": 1) Plurals are outlawed and 2) Adding a letter that could never possibly be a word is prohibited.
- Speak a letter and begin.
- Play as many rounds as fits your time, group, and program. Following is an example for five players and the leader:

    Leader: S

    Player #1: E

    Player #2: N

    Player #3: T (Here, the leader should point out that the game can continue as more words are possible.)

    Player #4: E

    Player #5: N

    Leader: C

    Player #1: E (Here, the leader should point out that there are no plurals allowed in this game, but the word can still go further.)

    Player #2: D

    Leader: Sorry, Player #2. Would you like to start the next round?

    Player #2: A

    Player #3: L (… and the game continues.)

Leadership Tip:

- Be aware that small words like *can* are certainly a complete word, but words like *can* could become, *candle, canopy, candy, cantaloupe,* and such.

#19: Word Association Challenge

Game Objective: To send a word pattern backward using a group memory challenge
Learning Objective: To improve command of the English Language
Recommended Ages: 12 to 112
Number of Players: 5 to 25
Energy Level: Low
Formation: Sitting in chairs in a circle
Props: None

Description:

- Begin by discussing with your group how word association is a commonplace tool of many psychiatrists. When the doctor says a word, the patient says the first word that comes into his mind.
- Inform your group that you are going to say a word, and the person on your right is going to say the first word that pops into his head. The next person on the right will respond to that word, and so forth around the circle.
- Let your group know that when the last person (the person on your left) speaks, play is now going reverse (i.e., to the left).
- Begin this backward round by saying the last person's word directly back to him. This player will have to say the word before his, and this pattern moves around the circle. Following is an example for six participants and the leader:

  Leader: Boy

Teller #1: Girl	Teller #6: Trouble
Teller #2: Mother	Teller #5: Grounded
Teller #3: Father	Teller #4: Father
Teller #4: Grounded	Teller #3: Mother
Teller #5: Trouble	Teller #2: Girl
Teller #6: Police	Teller #1: Boy
Leader (to Teller #6): Police	Leader: Good job, let's now try to go around two times.

Leadership Tip:

- Let your group know that besides picking up new vocabulary, this game puts the participants in the minds of another, albeit for a brief time. It is a gift any storyteller should appreciate.

#20: Word Convergence

Game Objective: To have two players in the group who have not consulted with each other to say the same word at the same time

Learning Objective: To improve word knowledge and selection

Recommended Ages: 12 to 112

Number of Players: 2 to 20

Energy Level: Low

Formation: Sitting in a circle

Props: None

Description:

- Begin by telling your group that this is one of the most complex games to explain, but it is well worth the time.
- As leader, think of a random word; truly any word in the English language will do.
- Tell your group that you will signal that you have thought of this random word by saying out loud the number, "One."
- Encourage another player to think of another random word and signal he has done so by stating the number, "Two."
- Indicate that when you say the number, "Three" out loud, both you and the other player will each state their random word simultaneously. Chances are it will not be the same word.

Stockbyte

iStockphoto/Thinkstock

- Alert your group that it is now their job to think of a word that connects those two words and once a person has done so, he should say out loud to the group, "One."
- When a second person thinks of a word that connects the two original random words, he should say out loud, "Two."
- Upon hearing the number two, the person who said, "One" will now say, "Three," and both players will state their word. Once more, chances are it won't be the same word, but the words will probably be closer in similarity, origin, or meaning.
- More rounds should be played until both players state the same word.
- An example round might look like this:

    Leader: One (meaning you have just thought of a word)

    Player #1: Two (meaning he has also thought of a word)

    Leader: Three

    Leader/Player #1: Banana/Penguin

    Player #2: One (He has thought of a word that connects those two words.)

    Player #3: Two (He has also thought of a word that connects those two words.)

    Player #2: Three

    Player #2/Player #3: Zoo/Fish

    Player #4: One

    Player #5: Two

    Player #4: Three

    Player #4/Player #5: Aquarium/Aquarium

    Leader: Good job, group. We did that in only three rounds.

Leadership Tips:

- Because of the complexities of this game, consider starting with an example round.
- If your group is large (more than eight people), once the rules are understood, you can separate your group into two teams and see which team can accomplish a Word Convergence in the least amount of rounds.
- This is a wonderful travel game.

#21: Proverb Remix

Game Objective: To guess reworded proverbs written by the group

Learning Objective: To improve vocabulary and word selection

Recommended Ages: 12 to 112

Number of Players: 4 to 40

Energy Level: Low

Formation: Sitting in pairs

Props: Pencils and scrap paper for every pair and one index card for the leader with the following proverb written on the card: "Refrain from numbering your barnyard fowl prior to their incubation."

Description:

- Read the index card, and have the group guess the reworded proverb. (Don't count your chickens before they hatch.)
- Invite the pairs to creatively rewrite another proverb of their own choosing.
- When each pair is finished, have them read their work aloud for the other groups to decipher and be the first to successfully guess.

Leadership Tips:

- It is generally helpful to have one or two other examples if the group is having difficulty, such as:
    - ✓ A spinning, dense, raw material will not adhere fungus. (A rolling stone gathers no moss.)
    - ✓ Engage your visual faculties prior to executing a jump. (Look before you leap.)
- Some examples of proverbs you might suggest for them to rewrite:
    - ✓ Every cloud has a silver lining.
    - ✓ The grass is always greener on the other side of the fence.
    - ✓ A new broom sweeps clean.
    - ✓ Every dog has its day.
    - ✓ It's always darkest before the dawn.

#22: Jack Codes

Game Objective: To be the first in the group to guess the Jack codes

Learning Objective: To see how stories such as Jack tales influence our lives.

Recommended Ages: 10 to 110

Number of Players: 2 to 30

Energy Level: Low

Formation: Sitting in chairs in a circle

Props: A stack of 8 1/2 x 11 sheets of paper with one Jack code per sheet written on the page in large marker. The Jack codes are as follows:

- JOL (Jack O'Lantern)
- JITB (Jack-in-the-Box)
- JITP (Jack-in-the-Pulpit)
- JOAT (Jack of all trades)
- JATB (Jack and the Beanstalk)
- JBNJBQ (Jack be nimble, Jack be quick)
- JSCENF (Jack Sprat could eat no fat)
- THTJB (The house that Jack built)
- JFDABHC (Jack fell down and broke his crown)
- JOH-JOD-JOS-JOC (jack of hearts, jack of diamonds, jack of spades, jack of clubs)

Description:

- Sitting in front of the group, hold up the first Jack code, explaining that "J" stands for "Jack."
- Explain that the participants want to be first to decipher and call out these popular phrases.
- Once the phrase has been guessed, continue through the stack.

Leadership Tips:

- You may have to give hints for the first one.
- You may wish to use these to decorate the walls of your class, workshop, or recreation space.
- An alternative way to play is this game it to have the Jack codes posted around the room before people arrive and have the participants solve them as they show up.
- You don't have to stop with these Jack codes. There are plenty more phrases that use "Jack."

#23: Two-Brain "Palinilap" (aka Palindromes)

Game Objective: To guess the palindromes others have created from the clues given
Learning Objective: To enhance the skills of creativity, imagination and word selection
Recommended Ages: 16 to 116
Number of Players: 4 to 24
Energy Level: Low
Formation: Sitting in distinct pairs
Props: Index cards and writing implements as needed by the pairs

Description:

- Begin this game with the explanation of a palindrome (or perhaps more appropriately, the authors prefer using the word "palinilap"): a word, phrase, or sentence that reads the same backward as well as forward. Some well-known palindromes include: "civic," "kayak," "top spot," "revolt lover," "max exam," "Never odd or even," "Rise to vote, sir," "Was it a cat I saw?" "Do geese see God?" and so forth.
- Allow each pair of participants about five minutes to create their own palindrome. You may wish to let your group know that palindromes are difficult to create, and it is acceptable in this game if they share one they already know.
- When everyone is ready, explain to the groups that they will present their palindromes in the following manner of question: "What do you call someone who loves tuna? Tuna nut." "What do you call intelligent male sheep? Smart rams." "What does a large jungle cat put in its mane to keep it looking nice? Lion oil."
- As each pair presents their questions, allow the others to guess the coinciding palindrome.
- Continue the game until all the pairs have shared their creations.

Leadership Tips:

- In this book, and in storytelling, there are palindromes, spoonerisms, portmanteaux, and hinky pinkys. As leader, you should be familiar with all four (thankfully, we cover all four in this book). Encourage your group to be extra patient with palindromes, they are the most difficult to create.
- Depending on your group, it sometimes works best to give out the palindrome, and let the group figure out the clue or question to go with it.
- As leader, it is a good idea to always have some nice examples in your back pocket. Following are some extra palindromes to help when needed:

- ✓ Senile felines
- ✓ Tube debut
- ✓ Stack cats
- ✓ Stunt nuts
- ✓ Tangy gnat

- ✓ Reward drawer
- ✓ Stressed desserts
- ✓ Wet stew
- ✓ Dumb mud
- ✓ Llama mall

- ✓ Bursitis rub
- ✓ Evil olive
- ✓ Dr. Awkward
- ✓ My gym
- ✓ Step on no pets.

#24: Two-Brain Phrase Craze (aka Hinky Pinkys)

Game Objective: To guess the proper phrase craze that other teams have created

Learning Objective: To improve skills of creativity, imagination, word selection, and command of the English language

Recommended Ages: 12 to 112

Number of Players: 4 to 24

Energy Level: Low

Formation: Sitting in distinct pairs

Props: Index cards and writing instruments for any group that needs them

Description:

- Explain that a phrase craze is an answer to a clue, riddle, or definition that is two rhyming words. For example, a large vehicle immobilized in mud would be a "stuck truck."
- Divide your group into pairs, and invite them to create their own phrase craze.
- When the pairs are finished, invite one pair to read just the clue or definition to the group.
- Allow the other participants to guess the two-word phrase craze.
- Once the correct rhyming answer has been guessed, continue the game until all the pairs have had a chance to present.

Leadership Tip:

- Some other examples you may wish to share:
  - ✓ A Jack O'Lantern carved to look like a hillbilly—Bumpkin pumpkin
  - ✓ A knitted wool shirt or blouse of high quality—Better sweater
  - ✓ Someone who makes fun of secured, metal containers—Locker mocker
  - ✓ A person who repairs swirling kitchen devices—Mixer fixer
  - ✓ A device that warms your bread and holds your beverage—Toaster coaster

#25: Two-Brain "Roonerspisms" (aka Spoonerisms)

Game Objective: To guess the spoonerisms created by the other groups

Learning Objective: To improve the skills of creativity, imagination, word selection, and command of the English language

Recommended Ages: 12 to 112

Number of Players: 4 to 24

Energy Level: Low

Formation: Seated in pairs

Props: Index cards and writing instruments for any pair that wishes them

Description:

- Begin this game with a small explanation of spoonerisms and how they often delight audiences when used well in a story. A spoonerism is a transposition of sounds between or within one, two, or more words. "Family" would be a "lamify," a "dark cloud" would be a "clark doud," or a "sliver of pie" would be a "piver of sly." Remember, it is a change of sounds, not letters. A "red table" would be a "ted rable," and so forth.

- You may wish to explain to your group that spoonerisms are named after a British cleric named Reverend William Spooner, who, according to legend, frequently "wixed-up his merds."

- Explain that there exists a unique kind of spoonerism which works in both directions. For example, a market that sells waterfowl can be paired with a hinged fixture that doesn't open (i.e., a "duck store" and a "stuck door").

- Place your group in pairs. Let each pair know that they need to each create one of these special spoonerisms and two short, defining clues to go along with it.

- In turn, have each group read just the clues while the other groups guess the spoonerism.

- Continue play until each group has had a turn.

Leadership Tips:

- Depending on your group, it might be helpful to have spoonerisms already on cards, and have your pairs just come up with the clues.

- Some other good examples of these special spoonerisms:
  - ✓ Big fan/Fig ban
  - ✓ Take a shower/Shake a tower
  - ✓ Crushing blow/Blushing crow
  - ✓ Battleships and cruisers/Cattleships and bruisers
  - ✓ Busy dean/Dizzy bean
  - ✓ Coffee table/Toffee cable
  - ✓ Tote bag/Boat tag
  - ✓ Hole puncher/Pole huncher
  - ✓ Butterfly/Flutter by
  - ✓ Jitterbug/Bitter jug

#26: Two-Brain "Twords" (aka Portmanteaux)

Game Objective: To guess from the clues given, the correct portmanteau

Learning Objective: To challenge our skills of creativity, imagination, word selection, and command of the English language

Recommended Ages: 12 to 112

Number of Players: 4 to 24

Energy Level: Low

Formation: Sitting in pairs

Props: Index cards and writing implements as needed by the pairs

Description:

- Begin this game with an explanation of a portmanteau, or as the authors like to call it, a "Tword" (i.e., the running together of two words to create a new word). Some common examples include: spork, brunch, smog, chunnel, and motel.
- Explain that it is the job of the pairs to create as many new portmanteaux as possible, creations with a question similar to the following, "What do you call it when you are jogging and juggling at the same time? Clearly, it's joggling." "What do you get when you cross a donkey and a chimpanzee? It might be a chimpanzonkey." "What do you call a person who is a Democrat *and* a Republican? A Republicrat."
- After two or three minutes, allow the groups to share their new portmanteaux. Continue the game until all groups have shared their questions and portmanteaux.

Leadership Tip:

- Some groups might need longer than two or three minutes for their creations. Tailor your time to fit your group and situation.

#27: Keyboard Olympics I

Game Objective: To be the first keyboard Olympian to fill out his blank keyboard

Learning Objective: To tap the powers of observation and recollection

Recommended Ages: 10 to 110

Number of Players: 3 to 30

Energy Level: Low

Formation: Sitting at tables or randomly seated with something to bear down on for writing

Props: A writing instrument and a plain, blank piece of 8 1/2 x 11 paper for each Olympian

Description:

- Instruct players to lay their papers flat and turn them sideways ("landscape"). Explain that they will draw three rows of roughly inch-in-diameter circles across. The top row will have 10 circles. Evenly spaced underneath those, the middle row will have nine circles. Evenly spaced under that, the bottom row will have seven circles. It should look similar to the following diagram.

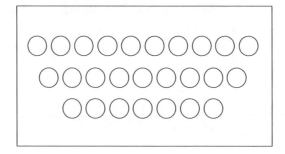

- Explain to your group that they are now staring at a blank, letters-only keyboard, and on your call they will be in a race to be the first to correctly fill in all the letters.
- Let players know that when they have finished, they should hold their page up high to acknowledge their accomplishment.
- Congratulate the first three finishers as your gold, silver, and bronze winners.

Leadership Tip:

- Encourage everyone to finish and hold on to the paper as it can be used for more word games.

#28: Keyboard Olympics II

Game Objective: To be the first Olympian to discover what is unique about three seemingly random words

Learning Objective: To test powers of observation

Recommended Ages: 10 to 110

Number of Players: 3 to 30

Energy Level: Low

Formation: Sitting in chairs

Props: An easel or dry-erase wipe-off board. Each player should have for reference his correctly filled out paper keyboard from Keyboard Olympics I.

Description:

- Begin the event by writing in large letters on the wipe-off board/easel the following words:
  - ✓ Stewardesses
  - ✓ Lollipop
  - ✓ Typewriter
- Explain to the group that they must be first to explain what is unique about these three words in terms of a keyboard.
- Congratulate your group on figuring out that "stewardesses" is the longest English word you can type with just your left hand, "lollipop" is the longest you can type with your right hand, and "typewriter" is the longest word you can type using just the top row of your keyboard.

Leadership Tips:

- After a short while, give the hint that the clues are on their paper keyboards.
- You can play this game without the paper keyboard but it is much more difficult.

#29: Keyboard Olympics III

Game Objective: To be the first Olympian to figure out what is unique about two words

Learning Objective: To test powers of observation and improve command of the English language

Recommended Ages: 10 to 110

Number of Players: 3 to 30

Energy Level: Low

Formation: Sitting in chairs

Props: An easel of newsprint or a dry-erase, wipe-off board, and paper keyboards from Keyboard Olympics I

Description:

- In large, bold letters, write the following two words on your wipe-off board/easel:
  - ✓ Abstemious
  - ✓ Facetious
- Explain to your group that they need to be the first to figure out what is unique about spelling or typing these two words.
- Congratulate the winner for being the first to know that all five vowels in these rare words are present *and* appear in order.

Leadership Tip:

- Give bonus points to the player who knows the definition of these two words:
  - ✓ Abstemious: eating, drinking, or any activity in moderation
  - ✓ Facetious: not speaking or taking what is spoken seriously

#30: Keyboard Olympics IV

Game Objective: To be the first player to guess a letter combination

Learning Objective: To encourage creative thinking with words and expand command of the English language

Recommended Ages: 10 to 110

Number of Players: 3 to 30

Energy Level: Low

Formation: Sitting in chairs

Props: Paper keyboards from Keyboard Olympics I and wipe-off board or easel of newsprint

Description:

- Before playing, write the following words on the board/easel:
  1. Vacant
  2. Not Difficult
  3. Snake's eyes
  4. Rot
  5. Chilly
  6. Too much
- Starting with the first word, move through the list asking the group, "Who can use their keyboard in front of them to find two letters that mean vacant?"
- Once the correct answer is given (M-T), congratulate that player, and move to the next word.
- Complete the list, giving lots of praise to all the participants.

Leadership Tip:

- As always, make sure you know the answers ahead of time (1. M-T, 2. E-Z, 3. B-D, 4. D-K, 5. I-C, 6. X-S), and invite your group to think of and share their own puzzle creations.

#31: Keyboard Olympics V

Game Objective: To be the first to discover what is unusual about an unusual word

Learning Objective: To challenge powers of observation

Recommended Ages: 15 to 115

Number of Players: 3 to 30

Energy Level: Low

Formation: Sitting in chairs

Props: A white, dry-erase, wipe-off board or easel with pad of newsprint and paper keyboard from Keyboard Olympics I for reference

Description:

- Explain to your group that this is the most difficult challenge of the keyboard Olympic events.
- Write the word "Triennially" on the board in large letters.
- Invite the group to study this word and their keyboards to discover what is unusual about this word in terms of a keyboard.
- Congratulate the player who discovers that you can type every other letter in this 11-letter word and still get another whole word whether you are typing every odd letter or every even letter. The odd letters give you "tinily." The even letters give you "renal."

Leadership Tip:

- Give bonus points to whoever can correctly define these three words:
  - ✓ Triennially: occurring every three years
  - ✓ Tinily: to a small or minute degree
  - ✓ Renal: of or near the kidneys

#32: Whiteboard Olympics I

Game Objective: To be the first player to figure out what a set of words have in common

Learning Objective: To enrich skills of creativity, observation, and imagination

Recommended Ages: 12 to 112

Number of Players: 2 to 50

Energy Level: Low

Formation: Seated so that everyone can see the whiteboard

Props: Whiteboard and dry-erase marker

Description:

- Write in large letters the following four words on your whiteboard: Banana, Dresser, Grammar, and Potato.
- Challenge your participants to be the first to shout out what these four words have in common.
- Congratulate the player who yelled out that all four words can be spelled backward if you move the first letter to the end.

Leadership Tip:

- Whiteboard Olympics are a wonderful way to begin any work/play session as they get groups actively thinking.

#33: Whiteboard Olympics II

· *Game Objective:* To be the first player to decide which word does not belong from a small list of words

Learning Objective: To enhance creativity, imagination, observation, and command of the English language

Recommended Ages: 12 to 112

Number of Players: 2 to 50

Energy Level: Low

Formation: Sitting so that everyone can see the whiteboard

Props: Whiteboard and dry-erase marker

Description:

- With your group watching, write the following words on your whiteboard in large letters: Binoculars, Jeans, Pliers, Scissors, Shoes, and Tweezers.
- Encourage your players to be the first to shout out which word does not belong.
- Congratulate the player who first recognized that shoes are the only pair listed that work best when they are not connected.

Leadership Tip:

- Don't forget that these Whiteboard Olympics are great for getting "blood flowing to the brain" and waking groups up first thing in the morning or directly after lunch.

#34: Whiteboard Olympics III

Game Objective: To be the first player to recognize the unique characteristic a list of words have in common

Learning Objective: To develop skills of creativity, imagination, observation, and command of the English language

Recommended Ages: 12 to 112

Number of Players: 2 to 50

Energy Level: Low

Formation: Sitting so that everyone can see the whiteboard

Props: Whiteboard and dry-erase marker

Description:

- With your group watching, write the following five words on the board in large letters: About, Bring, Drag, Equality, and Fox.
- Encourage your players to be the first player to shout out what these words have in common.
- Congratulate the player who first recognizes that you can drop the first letter of each word and still have a perfectly good word.

Leadership Tip:

- If the group is slow in solving this puzzle, nonchalantly begin writing more of the following words on your board: Ground, Hill, Irate, Know, Late, Mat, Never, Opinions, Part, Roar, Strait, Table, Vindicate, Washes, Your, and Zone.

#35: Whiteboard Olympics IV

Game Objective: To be the first player to recognize patterns in numbers that have little or nothing to do with them being numbers and everything to do with being words

Learning Objective: To practice skills of language, creativity, imagination, and observation

Recommended Ages: 12 to 112

Number of Players: 2 to 50

Energy Level: Low

Formation: Sitting so that everyone can see the whiteboard

Props: Whiteboard, dry-erase marker, and eraser

Description:

- Explain to your group that they are tasked to find word-related patterns in groups of numbers. There will be three distinct rounds.
- With your group watching, write the following numbers on your board: 1, 7, 11, 27, 77, 117.
- Invite your players to be the first to shout out what pattern these numbers follow.
- Congratulate the player who lets you know these six numbers are arranged by number of syllables.
- Wipe off your board for a slightly more difficult Round Two.
- Write the following numbers on your board: 73, 12, 6, 3, 5
- Ask your group to be the first player to shout out the unique pattern for this set of numbers.
- Congratulate the player who first lets you know that each succeeding number is the number of letters in the previous number.
- As an extra challenge, invite your group to tell you what the last number in this pattern will be and *always* will be no matter which number you start with.
- Offer more congratulations to the player who tells you, "Four."
- Wipe off your board for an even more challenging Round Three.
- Write the following large number on the board: 8,549,176,320.
- Invite the members of your group to be the first player to shout out the pattern found in this very large number.
- Congratulate the player who figured out that all the individual numbers in this much larger number are in alphabetical order. Congratulate the group for their participation.

Leadership Tips:

- As a clue, let them know that as a storyteller, you do not necessarily teach math, but you *do* teach words, alphabets, letters, and syllables.
- The hint "Say the numbers out loud" may help groups that become frustrated.
- For really stuck groups, write the numbers out using the words that represent them (e.g., "one," "seven," "eleven").

#36: Whiteboard Olympics V

Game Objective: To be the first player to figure out the next letter in a sequence of letters

Learning Objective: To improve skills of creativity, imagination, and observation

Recommended Ages: 12 to 112

Number of Players: 2 to 50

Energy Level: Low

Formation: Sitting so that everyone can see the whiteboard

Props: Whiteboard, dry-erase marker, and eraser

Description:

- Explain to your group that this game will be played in two rounds.
- Write on your board the following 11 letters: F T F T T T T F F F F.
- Invite your players to be the first player to figure out what letter should come next.
- Congratulate the winner for knowing that "S" (standing for 60) is the next letter. The sequence is the first letter of the numbers you need to count by fives.
- Erase the board in preparation for Round Two.
- Write the following five letters on your board: F S T F F.
- Once more, invite your players to be the first player to figure out what letter should come next.
- Applaud the winner for knowing that "S" wins again as it stands for "sixth," just as the other letters stand for their numbered places.

Leadership Tip:

- If any group is having trouble with these puzzles, give the following hints:
  - ✓ The letters have something to do with numbers.
  - ✓ Write the next letter in the sequence, and ask them to tell you *why* the correct answer is the letter "S."
  - ✓ If they are really stumped, begin to write the word that corresponds with the first letter, and so on.

#37: Whiteboard Olympics VI

Game Objective: To be the first player to solve a two-word puzzle
Learning Objective: To challenge skills of creativity, imagination, and observation
Recommended Ages: 12 to 112
Number of Players: 2 to 50
Energy Level: Low
Formation: Sitting so that everyone can see the whiteboard
Props: Whiteboard and dry erase marker

Description:

- With your group watching, write the following two words in large letters: New Door.
- While holding your marker up in front of the group, explain that the winner will be the first person to figure out the puzzle in his head, race forward, take the marker and write the correct answer on the board.
- To begin the game, state the following: "Please rearrange the letters in 'New Door' to make one word."
- Commend the creativity of the winner who raced to the board and wrote: "One Word."

iStockphoto/Thinkstock

#38: Whiteboard Olympics VII

Game Objective: To be the first player to figure out what five words have in common

Learning Objective: To sharpen skills of language, creativity, imagination, and observation

Recommended Ages: 12 to 112

Number of Players: 2 to 50

Energy Level: Low

Formation: Sitting so that everyone can see the whiteboard

Props: Whiteboard and dry-erase marker

Description:

- As your group watches, write the following five words on the whiteboard in large letters: Bring, Buy, Catch, Fight, and Seek.
- Challenge your players to figure out what these words have in common.
- Offer kudos to the first player who lets the group know that when in their past tense, all these words rhyme.

Leadership Tips:

- If the group is having difficulty with this puzzle, add the words "Teach" and "Think" to your whiteboard.
- A clue might be to encourage them to think about these words as if they happened yesterday.

#39: Whiteboard Olympics VIII

Game Objective: To be the first player to decipher which word does not belong in a list of seven words

Learning Objective: To polish skills of creativity, imagination, and observation

Recommended Ages: 12 to 112

Number of Players: 2 to 50

Energy Level: Low

Formation: Sitting so that everyone can see the whiteboard

Props: Whiteboard and dry-erase marker

Description:

- With the players watching, write the following seven words on the whiteboard in large letters: Dog, Foot, House, Line, Plate, Panda, and Seat.
- Commend the player who distinguishes himself by pointing out that all these words become new words or concepts when preceded by the word *Hot*, except, of course, for Panda.

iStockphoto/Thinkstock

#40: Whiteboard Olympics IX

Game Objective: To work as a group and make six distinct words out of four letters
Learning Objective: To test skills of language, creativity, imagination, and observation
Recommended Ages: 12 to 112
Number of Players: 2 to 50
Energy Level: Low
Formation: Sitting so that everyone can see the whiteboard
Props: Whiteboard and dry-erase marker

Description:

- Write the following letters on your whiteboard: O, P, S, T.
- Below these letters, on the left side, vertically number your whiteboard from one to six.
- Your board should look like the following example.

	O	P	S	T
1.				
2.				
3.				
4.				
5.				
6.				

- Challenge your group to call out six different four-letter words that contain each of these four letters.
- Write in the words on the whiteboard as the group calls them out.
- Commend your participants on a job well done when you have heard and written the following words: post, spot, tops, pots, stop, and opts.

#41: Whiteboard Olympics X

Game Objective: To be the first player to figure out what a group of words have in common

Learning Objective: To activate skills of creativity, imagination, observation, and above-average understanding of the English language.

Recommended Ages: 12 to 112

Number of Players: 2 to 50

Energy Level: Low

Formation: Sitting so that everyone can see the whiteboard

Props: Whiteboard and dry-erase marker

Description:

- With your group watching, write the following words on the whiteboard: Shooting Star, Short Bread, Bald Eagle, Horned Toad, Firefly, and Ground Hog.
- Encourage your participants to be the first one to call out what these words have in common.
- Congratulate the player who first deciphered that these words are all misnomers.

Leadership Tips:

- You will want to finish this game making sure that everyone present knows that a misnomer is a misapplied or inappropriate designation.
- If your group is having trouble with the challenge, continue to write other misnomers on the board such as Woodchuck, Prairie Dog, Catgut, Peanut, Koala Bear, and Dry Cleaning.
- It is often fun to finish this activity by having your group share other misnomers they know.

3

Games That Primarily Teach the Skills Needed to Tell Stories in Front of an Audience

John Rowley

#42: Ka-Blam Name Game

Game Objective: To learn the names of the others in the group in a fun and unique way

Learning Objective: To test the skills of imagination, creativity, and enthusiasm

Recommended Ages: 10 to 110

Number of Players: 3 to 30

Energy Level: Low

Formation: Sitting in chairs in a circle

Props: None

Description:

- Announce to your group that it is time to learn names and practice sound effects.
- Briefly discuss with your group how comic strips, comic books, and even the old *Batman* TV Show had loud, dynamic sound effects.
- Allow the group about a minute to think of a sound effect such as *Ka-Pow*, *Splat*, or *Zowie* that matches the first letter of their first name.
- Let the group know that each person will introduce himself in turn, and reintroduce all the dynamic participants that came before.
- Begin the game by introducing yourself, and allow play to move around the circle.
- Example:

    Leader: Ala-Ka-Zam Anthony

    Teller #1: Ala-Ka-Zam Anthony, Ka-Bam Kevin

    Teller #2: Ala-Ka-Zam Anthony, Ka-Bam Kevin, Wokka-Wokka Wendy

Leadership Tip:

- To keep things interesting, change the direction of play in circle games. Sometimes start with the player to your left, or consider having participants switch chairs before starting a new game.

#43: Story Statue

Game Objective: To discover which human statue has changed
Learning Objective: To practice the skills of gestures and powers of observation
Recommended Ages: 10 to 110
Number of Players: 5 to 35
Energy Level: Medium
Formation: Standing in a circle
Props: None

Description:

- Invite your group to strike a frozen pose that states something interesting about them. (For example, a percussionist might hold imaginary drumsticks as if playing, a golfer may be pretending to putt, a cook might be chopping vegetables, etc.)
- Once everyone has created a pose that tells something about himself, go around the group and ask each person to explain their pose.
- With everyone in their poses, invite a volunteer to stand in the center of the circle with eyes closed.
- Once you are certain this person has his eyes closed, point to a second player and ask him to alter his pose but keep the same original idea. (For example, the drummer might be hitting different drums, the golfer might be driving instead of putting, the cook might change which hand the knife is in, and so forth.)
- Once the second player is set and frozen, instruct the volunteer to open his eyes and make three guesses as to who changed his statue.
- If you desire a second round, ask the statue who changed to be your new guesser, and continue playing.

Leadership Tip:

- This is an excellent "get to know you" game.

#44: Family Portrait

Game Objective: To work as a team to present an unusual family portrait
Learning Objective: To practice the skills of gestures and facial expressions
Recommended Ages: 8 to 108
Number of Players: 6 to 30
Energy Level: Medium
Formation: Standing in two groups, facing each other
Props: None

Description:

- Let the two groups know that they will be, in turn, posing for a family portrait.
- Instruct one group to close their eyes.
- Instruct the other group to gather close together and pose as an unusual family such as the rich and snobby family.
- Allow about 15 seconds for the group to achieve their frozen pose, and then invite the other group to open their eyes. 99% of the time, participants open their eyes and laugh heartily.
- Play a second round, having the people who just posed close their eyes while those who just had their eyes closed pose as a different family.
- Play as many rounds as your time or group's enjoyment allows. Remember to stop the game before the group gets tired of it, using the positive energy to fuel the next game.
- Following is a dozen unique families to get you started:
  - ✓ The hillbilly family
  - ✓ The cannibal family
  - ✓ The professional wrestling family
  - ✓ The cheerleader family
  - ✓ The pirate family
  - ✓ The caveman family
  - ✓ The underwater family
  - ✓ The North Pole nudist family
  - ✓ The Star Trek/Wars family
  - ✓ The superhero family
  - ✓ The Olympics family
  - ✓ The pickpocket family

Leadership Tip:

- Some folks are uncomfortable closing their eyes, and others (especially children) are tempted to peek, spoiling their own fun. For these groups, simply ask the guessing group to face away from the posing group.

#45: Five-Snapshot Story

Game Objective: To meet the challenge of telling a story in five snapshots

Learning Objective: To work with the skills of facial expressions, gestures, and advanced understanding of what comprises a story

Recommended Ages: 12 to 112

Number of Players: 2 to 50

Energy Level: Medium

Formation: Seated as an audience, facing a real or imaginary stage

Props: No designated props (but participants are allowed to use whatever items they find in the room or space around them)

Description:

- Before the game begins, chose an assistant who is going to work with you to create and practice a small play portrayed in five photographic snapshots. (Examples follow.)
- Stand in front of your audience with your assistant, and instruct your participants to close their eyes and keep them closed until they hear you say the word, "Open."
- While your audience has their eyes closed, pose still and statue-like with your assistant.
- Invite the audience to open their eyes by saying the word, "Open."
- Allow the group to view your frozen scene for a few moments and then say, "Close" for people to once more shut their eyes.
- Fix your second pose and say, "Open." Allow a few seconds for viewing and once more say, "Close."
- This pattern repeats itself until the audience has seen a complete story in five frozen scenes.
- Once the participants have seen your well-practiced example, divide them into random groups of two, three, or four participants.
- Let everyone know that their smaller group is going to create and perform their own five-snapshot story for the entire group.
- After about 10 or 15 minutes of individual group preparation, call each team up to perform their tale.
- Example Story #1: Boy and Girl Team
  - ✓ Photo #1: A boy prepares to "flick" the ear of an unsuspecting girl.
  - ✓ Photo #2: The girl silently screams in pain, holds her hurt ear, and glares angrily at the boy who holds his sides and laughs.
  - ✓ Photo #3: The boy's face is frozen with shock as the girl's hand is inches from smacking his face.

✓ Photo #4: The boy silently screams in pain, holds his hurt cheek, and glares angrily at the girl who holds her sides and laughs.

✓ Photo #5: The girl rests her head on the boy's shoulder as the pair look lovingly in each other's eyes.

- Example Story #2: Three Golfers (male or female)

  ✓ Photo #1: A serious golfer lines up to putt from about 12 feet away. Two friends stand near the hole. One friend holds the flag. Both friends should be staring at the distance to putt and smirking about how their friend has no chance of making the shot.

  ✓ Photo #2: The pair should be laughing and pointing at the imaginary ball which is four yards on the other side of the hole. The other golfer should be angrily squeezing his putter in a clear rage that his ball missed and his two friends are no true friends at all.

  ✓ Photo #3: This photo is an almost exact duplicate of Photo #1, just from the opposite direction.

  ✓ Photo #4: This photo is an almost exact duplicate of Photo #2, just from the opposite direction.

  ✓ Photo #5: One friend lays unconscious on the green. The other friend, on hands and knees, begs for the imaginary putter to not strike as the smiling golfer is gleefully poised to bring it down.

#46: Old Witch Died

Game Objective: To not be the player standing without a chair

Learning Objective: To practice gestures and especially facial expressions

Recommended Ages: 8 to 80

Number of Players: 10 to 50

Energy Level: High

Formation: Sitting in sturdy, armless chairs randomly place around the room (leader should be standing)

Props: Only the chairs

Description:

- With all the participants seated, teach the following three-part dialogue:

    Part One
    Leader: The old witch died!
    Group: How did she die?
    Leader: She died like this! (Here, you will contort your face and body into some, bizarre, unique, grotesque, funny, silly pose.)
    Group: She died like this! (Group imitates the pose.)

    Part Two
    Leader: The old witch died!
    Group: How did she die?
    Leader: She died like this! (Strike an entirely new pose.)
    Group: She died like this! (Group imitates the pose.)

    Part Three
    Leader: The old witch is *alive!*
    Group: Where is she living?
    Leader: She's living nearby and she's coming right *now!*

- Once your group has learned this easy chant, explain that on the next time you say the word "now," they will all be expected to get up and carefully run to a new chair.
- Loudly repeat the three-part chant, run to claim a chair (hopefully), and tell the last person standing that he is the new leader.
- Play as many rounds as time allows or is appropriate for your group.

Comstock

Leadership Tip:

- On the final line of the chant, it is fun to personalize this game to the setting you are in:
  - ✓ "She's living at Camp Albemarle and she's coming right *now*!"
  - ✓ "She's living at Makemie Woods and she's coming right *now*!"
  - ✓ "She's living beside Stonehouse Presbyterian and she's coming right *now*!"

#47: Alphabet Challenge

Game Objective: To successfully recite the alphabet as a group under strict guidelines
Learning Objective: To practice the skill of reading and negotiating with an audience
Recommended Ages: 12 to 112
Number of Players: 7 to 26
Energy Level: Low
Formation: Sitting in chairs in a circle
Props: None

Description:

- Before the game, count your number of players, and find the corresponding letter in the alphabet. (If you have seven players, the letter you need is "G." If you have 13 players, the letter you need is "M." Naturally, for 26 players, you would need the letter "Z.")
- Tell your group that they are going to recite the alphabet to the designated letter with each player shouting out one and only one letter.
- Let your group know that there are three important restrictions that will necessitate the game starting over at the beginning:
  ✓ Two players may not speak at the same time.
  ✓ A player may not shout a letter if they are sitting directly next to someone who just offered a letter. For example, if a player says "B," neither player on his right nor left may say "C."
  ✓ Besides stating letters, no talking or gestures are allowed.
- Once the rules are understood, say to the circle, "Group, let me hear your ABCs!"
- Watch and listen carefully to make sure the three restrictions are adhered. Any time there is a breach, be prepared to state firmly, "Group, let me hear your ABCs!" as the signal for the group to begin again with "A."
- Congratulate your group when they finally complete their task.

Leadership Tip:

- Some groups never make it to their assigned letter, and that is fine as well. Their good efforts should also be praised.

#48: Adverb Challenge

Game Objective: To guess the adverb that different teams are acting out

Learning Objective: To improve gestures, facial expressions, word selection, reading the audience, and advancing understanding of the English language

Recommended Ages: 10 to 80

Number of Players: 6 to 50

Energy Level: Medium

Formation: Sitting in chairs facing a real or imaginary stage

Props: None

Description:

- Place participants in teams of roughly five people per team—no less than three and no more than six.
- Ask groups to huddle together and choose a secret adverb.
- Once secret adverbs are established, call individual teams up to the stage area to demonstrate/perform/act out their adverb. Teams can act as one group or perform individually, but all perform at the same time.
- After about 10 seconds, encourage the audience to yell out adverbs until the secret adverb has been correctly guessed.
- After 15 seconds, if no one has successfully guessed the performing team's secret adverb, have the performing team shout it out.
- Continue the game until all groups have performed.

Leadership Tips:

- If you have a small group and only two teams, have the two groups face each other and go back and forth acting out their secret adverb.
- Some good adverbs to suggest include: quickly, sharply, crazily, frigidly, cautiously, sleepily, angrily, happily, sadly, slyly, cleverly, mysteriously, playfully, and whimsically.

#49: In the Style of Your Adverb

Game Objective: To correctly guess an adverb the group has secretly chosen

Learning Objective: To engage our skills of gestures, facial expressions, word selection, and advancing our understanding of the English language

Recommended Ages: 10 to 110

Number of Players: 2 to 24

Energy Level: Medium to high

Formation: Sitting in chairs in a circle

Props: None

Description:

- Have one volunteer leave the room as the group decides on an adverb.
- Call the volunteer back, and explain to him that he can approach anyone in the circle and ask that person to act out the chosen adverb by stating: "In the style of your adverb ..." (Here, the volunteer will include some task, motion, action, etc.) For example, the volunteer might say, "In the style of your adverb, scratch your head," "In the style of your adverb, play baseball," or "In the style of your adverb, wave to your friends."
- After an individual performs for the volunteer, he is allowed to make one guess as to what is the secret adverb.
- Allow the volunteer to make five guesses before revealing the adverb.
- Play as many rounds as is appropriate for your time and your group.

iStockphoto/Thinkstock

#50: I Don't Like the Consonant ...

Game Objective: To not answer a question with the letter a player dislikes

Learning Objective: To work on the skills of imagination, word selection, and understanding the English language

Recommended Ages: 12 to 112

Number of Players: 2 to 30

Energy Level: Low

Formation: Sitting in chairs in a circle

Props: None

Description:

- Go around the circle, and ask each person to name a consonant they dislike, or at the very least, do not like as much as others.
- After going around the circle, ask for a volunteer to stand.
- Explain that three members of the group will, in turn, ask the volunteer a question, which he must answer without using a word that *begins* with the consonant he has claimed to dislike.
- Example round (Person does not like the letter "M"):

    Questioner #1: What month comes after February?

    Volunteer: The third one.

    Questioner #2: What is the yellow substance you put on a hot dog?

    Volunteer: Cheese.

    Questioner #3: What does ice cream do in the sun?

    Volunteer: Dissolves quickly.

    Leader: Nice job, volunteer. Who else would like to try?

- Have players who would like to ask a question of the volunteer raise their hands. Select three people to ask their questions.
- Once a player has answered his three questions, invite him to sit and select a new volunteer.
- Continue the game until everyone who desires to be the volunteer has a turn.

Leadership Tips:

- If you know your group and you are certain everyone will want a turn, have your standing volunteer select the next player.
- If your group is slow to come up with questions, feel free to ask a few of your own to get their creativity going.

#51: Eye Contact

Game Objective: To remain in the game by not making eye contact with your neighbors

Learning Objective: To practice the fundamental skill of making eye contact with your audience

Recommended Ages: 8 to 108

Number of Players: 6 to 20

Energy Level: Low

Formation: Standing in a close circle without touching the other participants

Props: None

Description:

- Remind your participants of the importance of eye contact, especially with small audiences. Point out that this is one of the primary differences between theatre and storytelling. When two people make true, full eye contact, both realize what has happened.
- Direct participants to look at their shoes.
- Tell players, "Think of one other person in the circle and picture him in your mind."
- Explain that when you say, "Look up," they should stare directly at that person they pictured, *and* if the other person is clearly looking back, both move from the circle and enjoy watching the other participants.
- Repeat, "Look at your shoes" and then "Look up" until only two players remain.
- If you have a large group, invite the ones eliminated to start their own game off to the side.

Leadership Tips:

- This game is very useful if your next planned activity requires participants to be in pairs.
- An interesting variation to this game is to have the two players who make eye contact to scream wildly when that connection is made. It can be a little startling, but is a good skill builder for enthusiasm.

#52: Applause Meter

Game Objective: To find a hidden object
Learning Objective: To practice the skill of reading an audience
Recommended Ages: 7 to 70
Number of Players: 6 to 30
Energy Level: Medium
Formation: Sitting in chairs in a circle
Props: A small item (such as a die, coin, pen, this book, etc.)

Description:

- Ask for a volunteer to leave the room.
- Have a second volunteer hide the selected small item somewhere in the room.
- Instruct the group that when the first volunteer returns, the group will direct him to the hidden object with just applause. No words should be spoken.
- As you invite the first volunteer back in, let him know he must find the hidden object, using the group's applause as his only hints.
- Once the player has found the hidden object, allow him to select the next volunteer to leave the room, and then hide the object. Play as many times as your program, lesson plan, or time dictates.

Leadership Tip:

- As leader, reserve for yourself the privilege to give vocal hints if the person searching is not catching on too quickly.

#53: Just a Minute

Game Objective: To take a seat at precisely one minute
Learning Objective: To help understand the skill of tempo
Recommended Ages: 10 to 110
Number of Players: 2 to 80
Energy Level: Low
Formation: Sitting in chairs in a circle
Props: A watch delineating seconds for the leader

Description:

- Invite everyone in your circle to stand.
- Explain that, on your signal, they are all at the same time going to start telling any story they desire. After precisely one minute, without looking at any timepiece, they should sit back down and stop speaking.
- With your timepiece ready, state clearly, "On your mark, get set, tell!"
- As people begin telling, watch carefully for three people and their corresponding times: the teller who sat first, the teller who sat closest to or exactly on time, and the person who sat last.
- When all are finished, review with the group the times you noted. Most will not be as aware of how time passes while telling as they think they are.

Leadership Tip:

- Most tellers will agree that perhaps the biggest faux pas you can make as a teller is to run long and cheat the person who is next to tell.

#54: Textures

Game Objective: To travel from one end of a room to another, imagining the world is constructed from a single texture

Learning Objective: To actively test the essential skills of gestures, facial expressions, imagination, and creativity

Recommended Ages: 10 to 110

Number of Players: 2 to 20

Energy Level: High

Formation: Standing in a straight line at one end of a clear, open play area indoors or out

Props: Indoors, the finish line is simply the other end of the room; outdoors, you will need a finish line marker, a cone, a flag, a friend, or such

Description:

- Instruct participants to stand at one end of the play area in a straight line facing the designated finish line.
- Let your group know that this activity is not a race and is to be done without speaking. Yelps, moan, groans, and screams are fine when necessary, but no words.
- Offer your group the following scenario: "Imagine you are walking through sand barefoot so take a moment to recall what that feels like. (small pause) Now, like walking through sand barefoot, imagine that the air around you is sand—and not just the air, *everything* is sand. We live in a sand universe. Your task is to travel from one end of this play space to the other in our world of sand. Begin."
- After you have observed everyone carefully travel across the area, send them back with a different universe texture.
- Finish this exercise by asking what it was like to live in such a universe. You may wish to point out some interesting gestures and facial expressions you saw as participants moved across.

Leadership Tips:

- After a group has moved across your play area, you may ask if anyone would like to tell a story in this universe.
- You and your group are encouraged to be creative and think up different "textures" that would be interesting to your group.
- Texture examples that work well:

✓ Furry	✓ Slippery	✓ Peanut butter
✓ Hot or cold	✓ Fragile	✓ Bubbles
✓ Silky	✓ Gelatin	✓ Puppies
✓ Sticky	✓ Earthworms	

#55: What Are You Doing?

Game Objective: To challenge players to perform a specific action

Learning Objective: To practice the skills of gestures, facial expressions, and enthusiasm

Recommended Ages: 10 to 110

Number of Players: 4 to 35

Energy Level: Medium

Formation: Standing in a semi-circle with a large play space at the front

Props: None

Description:

- Stand in front of the group and let them know that on their turn, when they approach the person at the front, they should say loudly and clearly, "What are you doing?"
- Begin the pantomime of a common activity such as brushing your teeth, combing your hair, or washing your hands.
- Motion for the player closest to you, on your right, to approach you and ask the appointed question.
- If you are pretending to brush your teeth, you are not going to say, "I am brushing my teeth." Instead, you are going to state a completely different activity such as, "I am riding a horse," "I am driving a car," or "I am playing golf."
- The person who just walked up now has to begin doing the new activity.
- Once this new person has had a chance to perform for a few seconds, motion to the next person to come up and ask, "What are you doing?"
- Continue moving around the semi-circle until everyone has had a chance to perform.

Leadership Tip:

- The group will quickly figure out that the most fun in this activity is in making the person behind them do something completely silly or outrageous. This is fine, but as the leader, pay close attention that nothing inappropriate is suggested.

#56: This Is Not A ...

Game Objective: To create a new use for an ordinary object

Learning Objective: To practice gestures and facial expressions along with creation and imagination

Recommended Ages: 10 to 110

Number of Players: 5 to 30

Energy Level: Medium

Formation: Standing in a semi-circle with a small play area at the front

Props: Your choice of a common, everyday object (such as a tin can, a chair, a broom, this book, etc.)

Description:

- Before the game, choose your common, everyday object (such as a tin can).
- Stand in front of the group and state loudly, "This is not a tin can, this is ... (here you will creatively imagine the object as something entirely new) a drum," and as best you can, play your new drum as if it were an actual drum.
- Motion for the person on your right in the semi-circle to come forward, and take the object while you return to the group.
- Explain to the group that the player holding the object will now state, "This is not a drum ..." and once more reimagine the can as something new such as, "this is my steering wheel."
- After this player has "driven his vehicle" for a few seconds, motion for the next person to come forward and continue the pattern until everyone has had a turn.

Leadership Tip:

- Play as many rounds as your time and program allow.

#57: Hitchhiker

Game Objective: To unexpectedly take on the affliction(s) of a hitchhiker

Learning Objective: To practice the in front of audience skills of voice inflection, enthusiasm, facial expressions, and gestures

Recommended Ages: 10 to 110

Number of Players: 4 to 30

Energy Level: Medium

Formation: The group should be sitting in chairs in the formation of a semi-circle or an audience. At the front, four empty chairs are set up to look like the interior of a car.

Props: None

Description:

- Before beginning the game, explain to your group that the four chairs represent an imaginary car. For the game to work well, they will need to know how to place themselves inside.
  - ✓ The front passenger seat is the assigned place for the hitchhiker.
  - ✓ After being the hitchhiker for one round, the player will then move to the driver's seat.
  - ✓ After being the driver for a round, the player will move to the back passenger seat behind the hitchhiker.
  - ✓ For a person's last round in the car, he will be a passenger behind the driver and exit the car back to the audience when the round is over.
- Call for three volunteers to fill the driver and back two passenger seats as you stand outside the car as a hitchhiker, trying to get a ride. Let your group know that one of the rules of the game is that, unlike the real world, you always have to pick up the hitchhiker.
- Stand with your thumb out, and let the driver know he should pantomime stopping his vehicle to let you in.
- Once the car has stopped, open the door, extend whatever greetings you wish, take a seat, buckle-up and freeze the game at this point to give one final instruction: Explain that the hitchhiker will begin displaying some kind of problem or affliction (such as sneezing, coughing, babbling, talking too loudly, uncontrolled crying, etc.).
- Make it known that when the others in the car perceive the affliction, they all catch it too.
- Allow this chaotic scene to play out for about a minute and then yell, "Switch!" letting everyone in the car know the round is over, and they need to move to their new place in the vehicle.
- Invite a new person from the group/audience up to be the hitchhiker, and begin again.
- Play enough rounds so that the original three volunteers in the car all have their turn at being the hitchhiker.

Leadership Tip:

- This is the perfect game for the leader to demonstrate what participants need to do, as opposed to running the risk of overexplanation. Play the game, have fun, and your audience will too.

#58: Who Is That Knocking at My Door?

Game Objective: To figure out who is knocking when you can't see who it is
Learning Objective: To practice the skills of voice inflection and projection
Recommended Ages: 10 to 110
Number of Players: 5 to 25
Energy Level: Low
Formation: Sitting in chairs in a semi-circle with a small, open play area at the front
Props: A hardcover book and a soft blindfold, such as a bandana

Description:

- Before beginning, let your group know that this game works best with a blindfold, but anyone uncomfortable wearing a blindfold can simply close their eyes on their turn.
- Explain to your group that in this game they are going to have to know two short, but important lines of dialogue. Practice once or twice saying:
  - ✓ "Who is that knocking at my door?"
  - ✓ "One of Santa's elves, collecting for the poor."
- Ask for a volunteer to join you at the front.
- Ask the volunteer to close his eyes as you cover him with the blindfold, or let the volunteer blindfold himself.
- Hand the volunteer the book, and have him hold the book out in front of himself with two hands securely on the book's sides.
- By just pointing and using no sound, select another volunteer to come stand in front of the first volunteer.
- Instruct this new player to gently, with one hand or the other, "knock" on the book (the door).
- Let your blindfolded player know it is time to state the first line of dialogue: "Who is that knocking at my door?"
- Explain to this second volunteer that he should disguise his voice so that the blindfolded player does not know who he is, then have him say his line: "One of Santa's elves, collecting for the poor."
- After the second player says his line, allow the blindfolded player to make two guesses as to who this "elf" might be.
- If the guesser is correct, the elf becomes the new guesser holding the book.
- If the guesser is incorrect, silently call another player up to knock and say his line with his best disguised voice.
- Allow the blindfolded guesser three rounds to figure out who the elf might be. If he remains unsuccessful, graciously and gently retire the guesser and call for a new volunteer.

Leadership Tips:

- This game works best if the group has begun to know each other fairly well.
- This game leads well into a discussion on the idea that when you tell a story such as a fairytale, hopefully, your voices are distinct. Your elf should not sound like your troll, your princess should not sound like your witch, your giant shouldn't sound like your prince, and none of these standard characters sound like you.

#59: Describe and Draw

Game Objective: To describe a simple picture well enough for your partner to draw it
Learning Objective: To improve descriptive ability
Recommended Ages: 10 to 110
Number of Players: 2 to 22
Energy Level: Medium
Formation: Two lines of chairs facing away from each other
Props: Pencils, scrap paper, one dry-erase board, and markers on an easel facing one row of the chairs

Description:

- Place participants in teams of two, and have them sit in the chairs facing away from each other.
- Give paper and pencil to the team member facing away from the dry-erase board.
- Draw a simple picture on the board (such as a flower, house, sunset, etc.).
- Explain to the team members facing the board that they must describe to their partner the image on the board and describe it so well their partner can draw it without viewing it. Allow three to four minutes for describing, drawing, dialoguing, but no peeking.
- Have participants share their drawings with the other groups, and complete the round by having participants vote on the drawing that looks most like the original.
- After the voting, have team members switch seats and play a new round.

Leadership Tip:

- Keep the drawings simple. You may wish to practice your drawings beforehand.

#60: Rock, Paper, Scissors, Cheerleader

Game Objective: To win or cheer for the ultimate winner of a large game of Rock, Paper, Scissors

Learning Objective: To practice the skill of enthusiasm

Recommended Ages: 6 to 106

Number of Players: 8 to 80

Energy Level: High

Formation: Standing face-to-face in pairs

Props: None

Description:

- After you have the group in pairs, review the childhood game of Rock, Paper, Scissors.
- Make sure everyone knows rock is a clenched fist, paper is a flat hand with fingers together, and scissors are the first and middle fingers extended.
- Be certain that all participants know that scissors cut paper, paper covers rock, and rock smashes scissors.
- Play a test round where each pair, on their own count of three, throws out one of the traditional three hand symbols to either win, lose, or tie. (Tied players continue until there is a winner.)
- Explain that from this point on, the loser of a match becomes the "cheerleader" of the winner, who will seek out another winner to challenge. He should enthusiastically support this winner as long as this player keeps winning. Should this player lose a match, both the losing player and his cheerleader become cheerleaders for the new winner.
- Let the group know that a winner will keep gathering cheerleaders until only two winners are left and will challenge each other with the entire group screaming loudly for their champion.

Leadership Tips:

- The leader should play if there is an odd number of players.
- Encourage cheerleaders to cheer as loudly as they can for their champion.

#61: I Know a Word That Rhymes With …

Game Objective: To correctly identify the secret word by acting it out
Learning Objective: To improve gestures and facial expressions
Recommended Ages: 6 to 106
Number of Players: 2 to 30
Energy Level: Medium
Formation: Sitting in chairs in a circle
Props: None

Description:

- Introduce this game with the following scenario:

  When I was in first grade, our teacher would stand in front of the class and say, "I know a word that rhymes with cat." We all knew to raise our hands, wait our turn, suggest a word, and hopefully be the student to win her game by guessing her secret rhyming word. It might be hat, bat, spat, rat, or many others.

- Next, explain to your group that you are going to play that old game with one exception: After they raise their hands and are called on, they may not speak the word, but have to act it out *and* act it out so well that the leader can tell what the word is.

- After the correct rhyming word has been acted out and acknowledged, let the player who was correct start the next round.

- Example:

  Leader: I know a word that rhymes with tree.

  Guesser #1: Is it a … (pretends he is a bee)?

  Leader: No, I'm sorry. It's not a bee.

  Guesser #2: Is it a … (pretends to strap a ski on his foot and go skiing)?

  Leader: No, I'm sorry. It's not a ski.

  Guesser #3: Is it … (pretends to be overjoyed)?

  Leader: Yes, it's glee. Good job! Would you like to start the next round?

#62: Triple Statement Lie Detector

Game Objective: To detect which of a player's statements is not true
Learning Objective: To practice all the skills we need in front of an audience
Recommended Ages: 10 to 110
Number of Players: 2 to 30
Energy Level: Low
Formation: Sitting in chairs in a circle
Props: None

Description:

- Invite your group to take a moment and think of two interesting, true statements about themselves and one statement that is a complete and total fabrication.
- Invite each person in the circle, in turn, to share his three statements.
- After each turn, poll players to see which statement they think is the lie, and then have the teller reveal the lie before moving to the next player.

Leadership Tips:

- As leader, you may wish to go first to set the example.
- As facilitator, be listening for which of the true statements might be hiding an interesting story. When the exercise is over, if time permits, ask the group if there were any statements they would like to hear more about.
- Some examples of interesting statements include:
  - ✓ I've been arrested four times.
  - ✓ I've got 11 cats.
  - ✓ My mother once worked for President Nixon.
  - ✓ I broke my arm playing checkers.
  - ✓ One time, I was sent to the principal's office for breaking the dress code.
  - ✓ I was kicked out of the College of William and Mary.

#63: What Would Your Face Look Like If … ?

Game Objective: To create spontaneous laughter in your group
Learning Objective: To practicing the skill of facial expressions
Recommended Ages: 6 to 106
Number of Players: 2 to 30
Energy Level: Low
Formation: Sitting in chairs in a circle
Props: None

Description:

- Explain that each person in the group, in turn, will say the phrase, "What would your face look like if … ?"
- Each player will finish the phase with something like "… you stepped in cow manure," "… you just kissed a pig," "… you ate an onion," "… you were giving birth," or "… you won the lottery?"
- Upon hearing the question, everyone should make their face at the same time for the enjoyment of the asker and the group as a whole.

Leadership Tip:

- This game works best if the leader goes first and with something simple, such as, "Group, what would your face look like if you had just been stung by a bee?"

Tom Raymond

#64: Cover Story

Game Objective: To figure out the peculiar characteristics of a ·group of criminal suspects

Learning Objective: To work on gestures, facial expressions, and descriptive ability while testing powers of observation

Recommended Ages: 12 to 112

Number of Players: 8 to 48

Energy Level: Medium

Formation: Seated audience-style with certain volunteers standing at the front

Props: A small stack of index cards prepared in advance with an unusual quirk written on the card

Description:

- Choose four or five volunteers as "criminal suspects" to stand before the group in a pretend police lineup.
- Hand one index card to each suspect to study for a few moments.
- Choose four or five volunteer "detectives" to stand off to one side or the other.
- Collect the index cards from the suspects.

Ryan McVay

- As leader, it is now time to show off your creativity and announce that some "horrific" crime as taken place, such as:
  - ✓ "Friends, last night someone broke into the local pharmacy and stole all of the acne cream. These suspects have been brought in for questioning."
  - ✓ "Ladies and gentlemen, this evening at approximately 8 p.m., someone snuck into Pizza Heaven and stole all the anchovies."
  - ✓ "Everyone, listen up. In the wee hours, early, early this morning, someone trespassed on the Makemie Farm and milked all of Farmer Makemie's goats, leaving them high and dry. The suspects stand before you."
- After a silly criminal scenario has been set up, invite the detectives to step forward and question the suspects. Each detective should have only one question (the same question) they ask of each of the suspects.
- Remind the audience that the suspects will all be answering in some unique or unusual way.
- When the questioning is finished, invite the audience to guess the quirk of each suspect.
- Following are 15 examples of quirks:
  - ✓ Always exaggerate your answers.
  - ✓ Answer with a different emotion each question.
  - ✓ Be evasive; never actually answer a question.
  - ✓ Always answer a question with a question.
  - ✓ Insert a compliment into every answer.
  - ✓ Rephrase each question before answering it.
  - ✓ Use each answer to flirt with the person asking the question.
  - ✓ Try to start an argument with each answer you give.
  - ✓ Always name a color in each answer.
  - ✓ Gesture with a different body part each answer.
  - ✓ Always use a number in your answers.
  - ✓ Answer each question as if you were George Washington alive today.
  - ✓ Always insult the person asking the question.
  - ✓ Use at least three hand gestures in every answer.
  - ✓ Exaggerate your facial expressions each time you answer.

Leadership Tip:

- To add one more interesting level to the game, have everyone present close their eyes and secretly select one of the suspects to be the actual criminal of your pretend crime. Finish the game by asking the audience to vote on who was the true criminal.

#65: Jungle Tales

Game Objective: To not be the last teller in the center of the circle without a chair
Learning Objective: To practice basic skills while telling an improvised story
Recommended Ages: 6 to 60
Number of Players: 4 to 24
Energy Level: High
Formation: Sitting in chairs in a circle with the leader standing in the center
Props: None

Description:

- Begin the game by placing your players into four fairly equal groups of jungle animals (e.g., lions, elephants, monkeys, alligators).
- Allow a minute or two for the groups to gather and create a motion and sound for their animals.
- Let the groups practice by demonstrating their sound and motion to the group.
- Ask the players to return to the chairs in the circle.
- As leader, begin an impromptu story about a jungle adventure, mentioning the different animals as you go.
- As each group is mentioned, they will perform their sound and motion.
- At some point in the story, the teller will yell, "Poachers!" and everyone sitting in the circle, plus the leader, will scramble for a new chair.
- One player will be left without a chair, and that person will become the new teller for the next round.

Leadership Tips:

- Know your group, and make sure you have a safe play area.
- Be inventive. You need not stick with the jungle theme each time you play. Suggestions can include farm life, parts of a car, creatures of the sea, trip through the desert, and such.

#66: Yes, Let's!

Game Objective: To behave and act as much as possible to match the group's suggestions

Learning Objective: To enhance the physical skills of gestures, facial expressions, and voice inflections

Recommended Ages: 6 to 106

Number of Players: 5 to 30

Energy Level: High

Formation: Standing in a circle with lots of room for movement

Props: None

Description:

- Before playing, let the group know that whenever a suggestion is made, the group will enthusiastically respond in unison, "Yes, let's!"
- Begin the game by making a suggestion with the following phrasing: "Let's all be …"
- Follow the word "be" with a suggestion of almost anything in the world (tigers, cars, fish, trees, clouds, waves, cowboys, toilets, chainsaws, etc.).
- After the group has exclaimed, "Yes, let's!" and performed your suggestion for about 20 to 30 seconds, allow the player on your right to make a new suggestion and continue the pattern around the circle.
- Allow each player in the circle to have his own turn making a suggestion.

Leadership Tip:

- Make sure your play area is free of any obstructions.

4

Games That Practice Telling Stories in Front of and With Others

George Doyle

#67: One Word at a Time Story

Game Objective: To pass a coherent story around the circle with everyone contributing

Learning Objective: To enhance the skills you need in front of an audience, plus the skill of word selection

Recommended Ages: 10 to 110

Number of Players: 2 to 30

Energy Level: Low

Formation: Sitting in chairs in a circle

Props: None

Description:

- Explain to your group that they are going to tell a round robin story. Each person will contribute just one word on their turn as the story is passed around the circle.
- Let the group know that at the story's logical conclusion, the last two players, whoever they are, will finish the story with the words: "The" and "End."
- Depending on the size of your group, you might need to go around the circle two or three times to get a complete tale.
- As leader, it is your responsibility to start the story with the first word.
- Example:

    Teller #1: One
    Teller #2: day
    Teller #3: Jack
    Teller #4: went
    Teller #5: to
    Teller #6: seek ...

#68: Rainbow Round Robin

Game Objective: To pass a coherent story around the circle

Learning Objective: To enhance the skills needed in front of an audience while stretching the skills of imagination and descriptive ability

Recommended Ages: 10 to 110

Number of Players: 2 to 24

Energy Level: Low

Formation: Sitting in chairs in a circle

Props: None

Description:

- Explain that you are going to begin an improvised story but will stop when your tale mentions a color.
- The teller on the leader's right will then continue the tale until he says a color.
- Continue this pattern until it reaches the player on the leader's left, who will finish the story.
- If the group is small, you may need to go around the circle more than once.
- Example:

    Leader: One day Jack went out to seek his fortune. He met a man selling a large brown …

    Teller #1: … turkey. Unfortunately, Jack had no money. He did empty his pockets and found a tiny, green …

    Teller #2: … cat. If you've ever owned a cat this color, you would never trade it away. Once Jack was offered 12 silver …

#69: Stop Letter Round Robin

Game Objective: To tell a group story not being certain when you are going to tell next
Learning Objective: To practice all the skills you need in front of an audience
Recommended Ages: 10 to 110
Number of Players: 2 to 24
Energy Level: Low
Formation: Sitting in chairs in a circle
Props: None

Description:

- Before the game begins, announce to the group a random letter to be your story's stop letter. (Often, the letter "b" is a good letter to start.)
- Begin telling an improvised tale, and stop when you reach a word beginning with your stop letter.
- Ask the person on your right to continue the story and stop when he hits the designated stop letter.
- Continue this pattern around the circle until everyone has told.
- As leader, you may need to tap into your creativity and finish the tale if the person on your immediate left does not.
- Example:
    Leader: Today's stop letter is "b." One day, on his way to see the king, Jack was carrying a large, brass …
    Teller #1: … trombone. Jack liked to annoy the king. What Jack didn't know is that the king had just purchased a big …
    Teller #2: … sister. It's not easy to purchase relatives, but …

#70: Jet Speed Autobiography

Game Objective: To tell your entire life story in 15 seconds

Learning Objective: To enhance all the skills needed in front of an audience and word selection skills

Recommended Ages: 12 to 112

Number of Players: 4 to 80

Energy Level: Medium

Formation: Standing in small, tight circles of four people to a group

Props: A watch or device for the leader that denotes time in seconds

Description:

- After placing your participants in small groups of four, encourage them to place their heads close together, similar to a huddle.
- Explain that they each will have 15 seconds to tell their entire life story.
- Ask the tallest person in each group to raise his hand. Announce this person as the starter.
- On your mark, the starter will begin telling his entire life story.
- After 15 seconds, yell, "Switch," and the person on the starter's right will tell his story.
- Continue this pattern until everyone in the group has told.

Leadership Tip:

- Depending on the total number of people in your larger group, small huddles of three or five people work as well.

#71: Fast Change

Game Objective: To keep the tellers guessing where the story is going next

Learning Objective: To practice the basic in front of the audience skills

Recommended Ages: 12 to 112

Number of Players: 4 to 24

Energy Level: Low

Formation: Sitting in chairs in a circle

Props: None

Description:

- Explain that they are going to tell a round robin story with everyone, in turn, contributing to the tale.
- Tell the person on your immediate right that he will begin the story. Inform him that at the end of one of his sentences, you are going to say the word "change."
- The teller should completely change that last sentence. Then, he will continue with the story until he once more hears the word "change."
- Indicate that you will say the word "change" a total of three times per player. On the third time, the next player on the right will change the sentence and continue the saga. The previous teller becomes the new change master. The game ends with the leader finishing the story and the person on his immediate left saying, "Change."
- Example:

    Teller #1: One day, Jack woke up hungry. He wanted some sausage.

    Leader: Change.

    Teller #1: He wanted a moose. Sadly, Jack was a bad hunter. He didn't know how to shoot a gun.

    Leader: Change.

    Teller #1: He had lost his slingshot.

    Leader: Change. (And switch. The next player on the right becomes the teller; the previous teller becomes the one to say "Change.")

    Teller #2: Jack was legally blind. He couldn't find his gun, slingshot, or even the door.

    Teller #1: Change.

    Teller #2: He couldn't find his clothes. (And so the pattern continues around the circle.)

Leadership Tip:

- For less advanced groups, it may be more helpful if you, the leader, say "Change" for all the players, allowing the tellers to simply enjoy the story.

#72: Jack's Alive

Game Objective: To keep a story moving when no one knows who is telling next
Learning Objective: To practice basic skills in front of an audience
Recommended Ages: 10 to 110
Number of Players: 6 to 30
Energy Level: Low
Formation: Sitting in chairs in a circle
Props: A working flashlight

Description:

- Pick two volunteers to stand outside the circle with their backs to the group.
- Explain that one volunteer will be in charge of saying, "Jack's alive," and the other will be in charge of saying, "Jack's dead."
- Let the group know they are going to be passing the flashlight around the circle until the first volunteer says, "Jack's alive." This is the signal for the person holding the flashlight to turn on the light and begin telling an improvised story.
- At some random point in the story, the second volunteer will state, "Jack's dead," signaling the person with the light to turn it off, stop telling, and continue passing the flashlight around the circle.
- The next person to be caught with the light upon hearing the words "Jack's alive" will turn on the light and continue the story.
- The pattern repeats until a complete story is told.

Variation:

- To ensure the most people get a chance to tell once, instead of one person getting caught several times, the leader can instruct everyone to stand at the game's beginning. Once a player is caught with the light, he sits after telling and no longer is passed the flashlight giving more people opportunities to tell.

Leadership Tips:

- This game is a tribute to the ancient, classic version, where tellers passed a stick with a burning ember around a campfire. If you were holding the stick when the ember went out, you lit the stick, passed it on, and became the new teller until the ember went out again on somebody else. It is not recommended you do this version unless you know your group very well and can be sure they will be careful while literally playing with fire.

#73: 26-Sentence Story

Game Objective: To tell a group story with unusual guidelines
Learning Objective: To build basic in front of audience skills
Recommended Ages: 10 to 110
Number of Players: 2 to 25
Energy Level: Low
Formation: Sitting in chairs in a circle
Props: None

Description:

- Let your group know they are going to tell a round robin story with everyone adding one sentence at a time.
- Explain to your group their particular sentence must start with a successive letter of the alphabet, and you will be starting the story with the letter "A"
- The person on the leader's right should say a sentence beginning with the letter "B," and so forth, around the circle.
- You may need to go around the circle more than once to make it to the letter "Z." Their creativity will be tested with certain difficult letters.
- Example:
    Leader: About 10 years ago, Jack left home.
    Teller #1: Before leaving, Jack packed a suitcase full of squash.
    Teller #2: Cantaloupes were just too heavy so he needed squash, but no underwear.

#74: Silly Sentence

Game Objective: To keep a story alive despite what the characters are saying

Learning Objective: To improve basic telling in front of an audience skills, plus dealing with the unexpected

Recommended Ages: 14 to 114

Number of Players: 6 to 24

Energy Level: Low

Formation: Sitting in chairs in a circle

Props: One index card or slip of paper and one writing implement per person

Description:

- Invite each participant to write a silly sentence on his card or slip of paper. Examples include:
  - ✓ "I like three different types of sushi on my pumpkin pie."
  - ✓ "The ghost has stolen our puffins."
  - ✓ "Your dog is in love with my canary."
- Once this chore is completed, instruct everyone to fold their paper over and hand it to the teller on their right, who keeps the paper folded and unread.
- Explain that the unread paper they are holding is the dialogue to the story the group is about to tell.
- Begin an impromptu tale, and when you reach the point where a character has to speak, pull out your paper and read it.
- Motion to the person on your right to continue the story and once more read their paper when a character speaks.
- Allow this pattern to continue around the circle until everyone has had a chance to tell.
- Example:
  > Leader: A good while back, the king called for Jack to come to the castle. When Jack arrived, the king said (reading from the paper), "Most geese cannot tango."
  >
  > Teller #1: Jack wondered if he was there to teach waterfowl to dance, but said to the king, "Your face has more craters than the moon."

Leadership Tip:

- Carefully watch the group as they will want to read their card ahead of time, which will ruin much of the spontaneity and many surprises.

#75: Roll Play

Game Objective: To complete a group story with each player assigned to use only a certain number of words

Learning Objective: To improve word choice

Recommended Ages: 10 to 110

Number of Players: 6 to 24

Energy Level: Low

Formation: Sitting in chairs in a circle

Props: One die (the larger the better)

Description:

- Instruct each player to roll the die one time and remember the number.
- Explain that their randomly assigned number is the number of words they may use when their turn arrives to contribute to the round robin story.
- Let the group know that they may have to go around the circle many times to get a complete story.
- As leader, roll the die, get your number and then begin the group story with your assigned number of words.
- Allow the tale to move around the circle until the story is finished.
- Example: Every teller has an assigned number. The leader rolled a four.
    - (4) Leader: Most days, Jack saw …
    - (2) Teller #1: … a large …
    - (6) Teller #2: … bear. It was tall and smelled …
    - (1) Teller #3: … like …
    - (3) Teller #4: … a nest of …

Leadership Tip:

- It helps players to count their words on their fingers as they speak.

#76: Last Name Etymology

Game Objective: To invent a tale that both entertains the group and explains the origin of a player's last name

Learning Objective: To reinforce the skills or imagination and creation

Recommended Ages: 12 to 112

Number of Players: 2 to 20

Energy Level: Low

Formation: Sitting in chairs in a circle

Props: None

Description:

- Begin this game by going around the circle and asking each player to share his last name.
- Allow the players about four or five minutes to create a story that explains the origin of their last name.
- Allow each person to share his tale. You do not necessarily need to go around the circle in order.
- When all are done telling, go around the circle with the following questions to vote on:
  - ✓ Who had the most original story?
  - ✓ Who had the most humorous yarn?
  - ✓ Who had the most outrageous story?
  - ✓ Who had the most likely tale?
  - ✓ Who had the most unlikely tale?
  - ✓ Who had the story you wish you could hear every day for the rest of your life?

Leadership Tips:

- Invent new categories for the group to vote on (most revealing, most shocking, grossest, most heart-warming, etc.).
- You are also not required to do last names. Do origins of first names, place names, pet names, favorite cartoon character's names, and such.

#77: Someone Famous

Game Objective: To discover which player is lying about meeting someone famous

Learning Objective: To develop the skills of creativity, imagination, and discovering personal stories

Recommended Ages: 14 to 114

Number of Players: 5 to 30

Energy Level: Low

Formation: Sitting in chairs in a circle

Props: None

Description:

- Suggest to your group the idea that most everyone has met someone famous.
- Ask tellers to mentally recall a time they met someone famous or invent a completely fictional tale of meeting someone famous.
- Once each player has his real or fictional meeting set in his mind, go around the circle and invite each to tell his tale.
- When all the tales have been shared, go around the circle a second time, and have the group vote on whether the individual's story was real or a clever fabrication.

Leadership Tip:

- Listeners often enjoy tales of meeting famous people.

Note: It was during the invention of this game years ago that Anthony began telling the story of how he met James Brolin, Jimmy Dean, Vice President Dick Cheney, and the Queen of England. This game is a proven winner.

#78: Three Stories, One True

Game Objective: To decide which of three tellers is telling the truth

Learning Objective: To practice all the in front of an audience telling skills with the bonus possibility of discovering new stories

Recommended Ages: 10 to 110

Number of Players: 6 to 36

Energy Level: Low

Formation: Group sits in a semi-circle with three empty chairs at the front

Props: Index card and pencil for each player

Description:

- Make sure every player has an index card and writing instrument.
- Instruct everyone to write the following:
  - ✓ On the front side, write something interesting or unique that happened that most people in the group do not know about.
  - ✓ On the flip side of the card, print their name in large letters.
- Collect the cards, pull three at random, and invite those three people to the three chairs in the front.
- Quickly, read all three cards and choose the one that has the potential for the most interesting story.
- Stand in front of the three tellers and say, "You are now going to each tell, in turn, about the time this happened … (read the chosen card)." The two whose story was not selected will quickly create a tale based on the story from the chosen card.
- When all three have told, have the audience vote on who was telling the truth about what was written on his card.
- Finish the round by congratulating the "liars" on how well they fabricated, and the "truth teller" on how well he told his story.
- Call up three more tellers, and begin again.

Leadership Tips:

- It is okay if your group does not divide evenly into groups of three. The game will also work if your final group of tellers has two or four participants.
- Examples of the types of stories you might select:
  - ✓ Tell us about the time you accidently hit a police officer.
  - ✓ Tell us about the time you were attacked by a duck.
  - ✓ Tell us about the time you forgot to pay for something.

#79: Weaknesses

Game Objective: To decide which player is telling a lie
Learning Objective: To discover hidden stories in weaknesses
Recommended Ages: 14 to 114
Number of Players: 4 to 24
Energy Level: Low
Formation: Sitting in chairs in a circle
Props: None

Description:

- Begin this game with a short discussion of the idea that everyone has a weakness. For Superman, it is kryptonite. For most of us, it is chocolate, desserts, coffee, soda, television, or such things. For migraine sufferers, it is often wine, cheese, or fluorescent lights. Truthfully, most of us have several weaknesses.
- Let your group know that in a few moments they are going to share, if willing, one of their weaknesses and a time they suffered because of that weakness. (Examples: I was so anxious to get my morning coffee I spilled it all over my new dress. I drank so much soda, I got sick. The chocolate I hid in my socks melted.)
- Invite the group to close their eyes.
- Walk around the outside of the circle and silently tap someone on the shoulder.
- Ask the group to open their eyes and explain to them that one of them has been secretly selected to make up a fictional weakness and weakness story.
- Invite everyone who wishes to tell a weakness tale to do so.
- Once everyone who wants to has told, go around the circle and ask each player as to who he thinks the weakness fabricator is.
- Finish the game with having the "liar" stand.

Leadership Tips:

- This game is for groups that know each other well and have a certain level of trust.
- After the game, you may suggest to the group that lots of good stories exist because of our weaknesses and are waiting to be discovered and told.

#80: Story Balloon

Game Objective: To keep a balloon in the air while telling a story
Learning Objective: To practice all the basic skills of telling in front of an audience
Recommended Ages: 8 to 80
Number of Players: 5 to 100
Energy Level: Medium
Formation: Groups of 5 to 10, standing in large circles around the play area
Props: A large, full, round balloon for each group with extra balloons close by

Description:

- After dividing your groups into circles of 5 to 10 players, hand each group a balloon and ask them to practice keeping the balloon in the air by tapping it—a game we've all played a million times as children.
- Once each circle has practiced, let them know they are going to tell an improvised tale with the teller being the last player to tap the balloon. That person will tell until the next player taps the balloon.
- Explain that there is no penalty for the balloon hitting the floor, but they should try to tell a completed tale without that happening.
- State loudly, "On your mark, get set, tell," and allow about five minutes for active play.

Leadership Tips:

- Let groups do as they wish with their story. If they want to start their story over or begin an entirely new tale when their balloon strikes the floor, that's fine. If they want to tell more than one story in their time, or never finish one story, that's fine, too.
- The goal is to have fun and practice skills. The looser you keep this activity, the more fun participants will have.

#81: Story Jumble

Game Objective: To discover the secret teller

Learning Objective: To practice the skills of gestures, facial expressions, and observation

Recommended Ages: 10 to 110

Number of Players: 10 to 30

Energy Level: Medium

Formation: Two equally numbered teams stand facing each other about six feet apart

Props: None

Description:

- After dividing the group into two equal teams, instruct each team to form a huddle and quietly choose a secret teller.
- After both teams have made their choice, have them stand facing each other. Select one team to go first.
- Announce a common, well-known tale, such as Jack and the Beanstalk, Cinderella, or Little Red Riding Hood. It is the job of the "secret teller" to tell this tale.
- Explain that, on your signal, the rest of the team will begin telling any story they wish, while the secret teller tells the assigned story.
- Just before saying, "Go," announce there is one more catch. All tellers will be mouthing (lip-syncing) their story. No one will actually be speaking.
- Yell, "Go!" and allow the group to tell for about 15 seconds, and then say, "Stop."
- Finish this round by standing behind each player of the telling team and allow the other team to vote who was the secret teller.
- After the secret teller has been revealed, it will be the other team's turn to tell.
- You may select a new story for the secret teller, but it is not necessary.

Leadership Tips:

- If you wish, this game can be repeated with everyone on a team speaking at the same time.
- If you wish to take this game to the expert level, allow only gestures—no speaking or mouthing.
- This game leads to some excellent discussion questions:
  - ✓ What impact do distractions have on our listening?
  - ✓ What impact do distractions have on our telling?
  - ✓ How important are gestures?
  - ✓ Why is difficult to communicate when everyone is talking?

#82: Story Toss

Game Objective: To tell a group story while playing catch
Learning Objective: To work on basic skills and fast thinking
Recommended Ages: 10 to 110
Number of Players: 4 to 44
Energy Level: Medium
Formation: Standing in a circle with participant's hands on their own hips
Props: An easy-to-catch object (a fuzzy ball, a stuffed toy, small pillow, etc.)

Description:

- Ask all players in the circle to place their hands on their hips.
- Explain to your group that you will toss the toy to someone in the circle. When the player catches the toy, he should add another sentence to the story and then toss the toy to another player.
- Indicate that once a player has caught and told, he should leave his hands at his side as a marker that he has already had a turn. The telling player should only throw the toy to someone who has his hands on his hips.
- State the opening line to an impromptu story, such as "One day, Jack went off to seek his fortune," then toss the toy to a player.
- Allow the soft toy and story to move about the circle until everyone has told.
- Encourage the last person to receive the toy to finish the tale, or to throw the toy back to you, so you can finish the story.

Leadership Tip:

- If the group is small, allow the toy to move around the circle several times before finishing the story.

#83: Story Yarn

Game Objective: To keep a story moving as dictated by a ball of yarn
Learning Objective: To practice the basic skills of telling in front of an audience
Recommended Ages: 10 to 110
Number of Players: 3 to 30
Energy Level: Low
Formation: Sitting in chairs in a circle
Props: A softball-sized ball of yarn with large knots tied randomly every two or three feet

Description:

- Hold up the special ball of yarn, and begin telling an improvised tale.
- As you tell, you need to unroll the string from the ball while starting a new ball.
- When you arrive at your first knot, stop telling and hand the two yarn balls to the person on your right.
- From your example, he will know to continue the story and to continue the rolling and unrolling.
- Allow this pattern to move around the circle until everyone has told.
- Encourage the last person to finish the improvised tale.

Leadership Tip:

- If your group is small, go around a second or even a third time.

iStockphoto/Thinkstock

#84: From the Villain's Point of View

Game Objective: To be the "Most Misunderstood" or "Most Wanted" villain

Learning Objective: To practice all the basic skills you need in front of an audience, plus looking at stories from different perspectives

Recommended Ages: 12 to 112

Number of Players: 2 to 12

Energy Level: Low

Formation: Sitting in chairs in a circle

Props: None

Description:

- Before the game, review with your group the importance of the villain in a story, and explore the idea that the most popular children's stories have a villain.
- Assign each participant a different story with a well-known villain.
- Allow each teller about 10 minutes prep time to explore telling their assigned tale from the villain's point of view. (Some participants may wish to do this away from the group, or write notes.)
- Call your group back together, and invite participants to tell their old story in this new way.
- After everyone has told, ask your group to vote on which villain was truly evil and deserves the title of "Most Wanted" and which villain deserves the title of "Most Misunderstood."
- Examples of stories you may wish to assign:
  - ✓ Cinderella
  - ✓ Little Red Riding Hood
  - ✓ Snow White and the Seven Dwarfs
  - ✓ Sleeping Beauty
  - ✓ Goldilocks
  - ✓ Jack and the Beanstalk
  - ✓ The Three Little Pigs
  - ✓ Robin Hood
  - ✓ Peter Rabbit
  - ✓ Hansel and Gretel
  - ✓ How The Grinch Stole Christmas
  - ✓ Dr. Jekyll and Mr. Hyde

Leadership Tips:

- As leader, you are encouraged to create lots of different awards to highlight the insights of the people in your group.
- Consider playing with well-known comic book, movie, and television villains as well.

#85: Firing Squad Story

Game Objective: To complete a story while not telling any of the five players who is speaking next

Learning Objective: To practice all the skills you need telling in front of an audience

Recommended Ages: 12 to 112

Number of Players: 5 to 50

Energy Level: Medium

Formation: Seated in an audience facing a real or imaginary stage

Props: None

Description:

- Divide your group into teams of five, and assign each team member a number (one to five).
- Call a team up in front of the group, and have them line up in numerical order, left to right, from the audience's point of view.
- Explain that when you call out a number, the person assigned to that number will begin telling an improvised story until you call another number for another person to continue the tale as seamlessly as possible.
- Inform participants that you will likely call the numbers out of sequence, the time per teller will vary, and an individual's number will probably be called several times.
- Start the game by shouting a number, then after a short while, call a different number.
- Make sure each player has a chance to tell at least once, and be listening to hear if the tale is coming to a logical end.
- Conclude the round by yelling, "Teller number (X), finish the story."
- After applauding the tellers, invite another group up in front to begin again.

Leadership Tip:

- Depending on numbers, you may have a group that has three, four, or six participants, and the game works just as well.

#86: Boiler Burst

Game Objective: To not be the last player standing without a chair

Learning Objective: To practice the 10 telling in front of an audience skills

Recommended Ages: 10 to 80

Number of Players: 10 to 50

Energy Level: High

Formation: Everyone sitting in a chair as part of a large circle of chairs, except for the leader who stands in the center of the circle with no designated chair

Props: One chair per player

Description:

- Explain that you will tell a story, and at some point you will say the words "boiler burst." Let your group know that when they hear the words "boiler burst" as part of a story, they need to get up and carefully run to a different chair while you try to "steal" a chair for yourself.
- Make sure your group knows that the words "boiler burst" must come together and in that order.
- Begin telling an impromptu tale that works toward the key words.
- When you say the words and everyone runs, attempt to grab a chair for yourself. Let the last person standing know he needs to begin a new story.
- Play as many times as best fits your program, time, and group interest.

Leadership Tips:

- Let your group know that the stories can be short and simple: "The other day at my house, the boiler burst."
- Stories can be more complex: "There was a man who owned two dogs. One was named Boiler, and the other was named Burst. They kept running off and rarely came back when called. The man would be on his back porch yelling, 'Burst, Burst, Burst, Boiler,' but they would never come. He would sometimes yell, 'Burst, Boiler, Boiler,' but they would never come. But one day he yelled, 'Boiler, Burst …'"
- Stories can also tease creatively: "Ray was a mechanic on an old steamship. He was in charge of keeping the boiler in good working order, but each day the boiler belched. Sometimes, the boiler burped. Sometimes, the boiler busted. Other times, the boiler burst …"

#87: Number Six Wins

Game Objective: To gain control of the story by rolling a number six on a die
Learning Objective: To practice all the skills you need to have in front of an audience
Recommended Ages: 10 to 110
Number of Players: 3 to 12
Energy Level: Medium
Formation: Standing around a table
Props: A large die

Description:

- Let the teller on your right know that, on your signal, he will begin telling an impromptu story. All players should pay attention to the story being told while the game is being played.
- Hand the die to the player on that teller's right, and instruct him to roll the die as soon as the person on his left begins telling. If he does not roll a six, he passes the die to the player on his right, and so on around the circle.
- When a six is rolled, the person who rolled the six takes over telling the story and the die passes to the player next player and around the circle. When another six is rolled, the rolling player takes over, and the pattern continues.
- State loudly, "On your mark, get set, tell!"
- When appropriate, instruct a teller to conclude the story.

Leadership Tips:

- As leader, you will need to pay particularly close attention to the tale because the person rolling may not be able to both listen and roll at the same time. It is your responsibility to keep them caught up. You may have to make statements like, "Jack just fell in a hole," "The bear's chasing the king," or "The Army is lost."
- Ensure that each player gets to tell. If the same players keep rolling sixes, pass the die only among those players who have not yet told.

#88: Roy G. Biv

Game Objective: To tell a completed story without knowing who is going to tell next
Learning Objective: To test imagination and oratory skills in front of an audience
Recommended Ages: 6 to 106
Number of Players: 3 to 7
Energy Level: Medium
Formation: Standing in a straight line facing the audience
Props: Seven shuffled, colored index cards (colors: red, orange, yellow, green, blue, indigo, violet)

Description:

- Match the number of cards to the number of players (if you only have four players, remove three cards). Assign the standing players a color based on the index cards.
- Select a card/color, then point to the person assigned that color to let him know he should start telling an improvised story, explaining he should work his designated color into the story as many times as possible.
- After that person has told for a short while and has the story going well, draw a different card, and have that person continue the tale.
- Repeat this procedure until all have told, and inform the last teller to finish the story.

Leadership Tips:

- This game also works for larger groups. Simply have seven tellers at a time go up to perform for the larger group. Play enough rounds until everyone who wishes to go may go.
- It may work best for your group of tellers to go through the colored cards more than one time in one story.

#89: Neckties

Game Objective: To create many different stories from the same premise

Learning Objective: To unite the skills of creation, imagination, and telling

Recommended Ages: 10 to 110

Number of Players: 2 to 20

Energy Level: Low

Formation: Sitting in chairs in a circle

Props: 20 different neckties in varied colors and designs with one solid color tie for the leader

Description:

- Before the game, set out for display the 20 different neckties in the center of the circle.
- Invite each teller to choose a tie that "speaks to him."
- Holding the solid-color tie, stand before the group and say the following: "A long time ago, in the Land of Neckties, all ties were the same color. There was constant trouble because nobody could tell anyone apart. One day, the tie you are holding left, had an amazing adventure, and returned totally different."
- Invite tellers to regale the group with how their tie returned different.

Leadership Tip:

- If your group is meeting over several days or sessions, this makes a nice "homework" assignment.
- This game can use up a lot of time. Limit story length to fit your schedule.

#90: Fortunately/Unfortunately

Game Objective: To keep a story moving where the extremes keep changing
Learning Objective: To sharpen basic skills and imagination
Recommended Ages: 6 to 106
Number of Players: 2 to 20
Energy Level: Low
Formation: Sitting in chairs in a circle
Props: None

Description:

- Alternating around the circle, assign each player to be a "Fortunately" or an "Unfortunately" The player on your immediate right should be a "Fortunately."
- Once every player knows his role, begin an improvised story that stops when something terrible is about to happen. Example: "One day I was walking down the road when an enormous tiger jumped of the bushes. It was clear the beast was angry and hungry. I covered my eyes as the beast leapt."
- Point to the teller on your right to continue the story starting with the word, "Fortunately." Example: "Fortunately, a bolt of lightning came down from the sky and burned the tiger to a crisp."
- Motion to the next teller to continue the tale with the word "Unfortunately." Example: "Unfortunately, the lightning set the woods on fire, and I had to run for my life."
- Continue play around the circle until everyone has told.

Leadership Tip:

- Before long, players will begin to top each other as you go around the circle. Be encouraging as they stretch their imaginations, and let the story go wherever it needs to go.

#91: Scars, Piercings, and Tattoos

Game Objective: To get to know other participants
Learning Objective: To find hidden or forgotten stories
Recommended Ages: 18 to 118
Number of Players: 2 to 30
Energy Level: Low
Formation: Sitting in chairs in a circle
Props: None

Description:

- There are very few people in the group or in the world who don't have a scar, piercing, or tattoo. Suggest to your group that behind every scar, piercing, or tattoo, there is a story.
- Invite participants to share the story behind one of his scars, piercings, or tattoos.

Leadership Tip:

- As always, know your group. Certain scars, piercings, and tattoos should remain private. Encourage modesty and maturity. This game is best for groups who already have established a level of trust.
- Be prepared to allow anyone to pass who feels uncomfortable sharing information about their bodies.

Brand X Pictures

#92: Word to Sentence to Story

Game Objective: To tell a complete story as a group while not being certain which word you are going to have to use next

Learning Objective: To enhance basic skills and imagination booster

Recommended Ages: 10 to 110

Number of Players: 4 to 24

Energy Level: Low

Formation: Sitting in a circle

Props: None

Description:

- Invite everyone in the circle to think of a secret, random word and keep it temporarily to himself.
- Explain that beginning with you, the group is going to tell a story, going around the circle to the right, one sentence per person. This sentence must include the secret word of the person on his left.
- Before beginning the story, turn to the person on your left and ask his secret word. Use that secret word in your opening sentence.
- The player on your right will ask for your secret word, then add the next sentence to the story.
- Play continues around the circle with each person taking a word cue from the person on his left.
- If the group is small, you may wish to go around the circle twice to get a complete story.
- Example of a six-player round:

    Teller #6 (on the Leader's left): Garage.

    Leader: One day, Jack walked out to his garage. Duck.

    Teller #1: For some odd reason, Jack kept his duck in the garage. Star.

    Teller #2: This was a magical duck that could fly from the Earth to any star in the sky. Cat.

    Teller #3: Jack knew of an evil cat planet, where litter boxes were filled with gold. Shelf.

    Teller #4: Jack flew to the evil cat planet on his magic duck and hid behind a shelf of cat food. Toe.

    Teller #5: An evil cat saw Jack's toe sticking out and pounced on Jack. Train.

    Teller #6: To Jack's surprise, his magic duck used to train as a ninja warrior and was able to defeat the evil cats as Jack scooped up the gold kitty litter to return to earth a rich man.

    Leader: The End.

#93: Draw and Tell

Game Objective: To create a group story from a stack of random pictures
Learning Objective: To improve all the basic telling skills plus imagination and creation
Recommended Ages: 10 to 110
Number of Players: 4 to 24
Energy Level: Low
Formation: Sitting in a circle
Props: Index cards and writing implements for all

Description:

- Make sure each participant has an index card and a writing implement.
- Explain to your group that most every person can draw at least one item that others can recognize.
- Ask your group to take about one or two minutes and draw a single, simple item on the card (rock, tree, bird, sun, house, flower, etc.) As leader, you should draw an item as well.
- When everyone has finished, go around the circle and invite each person to share his picture and identify the item.
- Collect the cards, shuffle them, and hand out one card to each person with the instruction that only the holder should look at his newly received card. It is okay if he gets his own, and it is okay of there is more than one of the same pictured item.
- Explain to the group that they are going to tell a round robin story, going around the circle to the right. Each person will contribute a single sentence that contains the item on his card. For small groups, you may wish to have them draw two pictures.
- Let the player on your left know it will be his job to finish the story.
- As leader, hold up your picture and begin the story. The person on your right tells next, and so forth around the circle.
- Lastly, congratulate your group on their creativity and imagination.
- A six-person sample round:

    Leader (fish picture): One day, Jack was hungry and decided to go and catch a fish.

    Teller #1 (cannon): At first, he dragged his favorite fishing cannon out of the garage but decided it was too heavy and went back for his fishing pole.

    Teller #2 (duck): Just then, a duck flew over Jack's head, and he went back for the cannon.

    Teller #3 (camera): Jack's neighbors were watching and ran inside to get their video camera, hoping to film something that would win them a million dollars on the show, *Fairyland's Funniest Videos*.

Zoonar/Thinkstock

Teller #4 (cat): What Jack did not know was that there was a cat sleeping in the barrel of his cannon.

Teller #5 (flower): The amazing video of a flying cat bringing down a duck did win Jack's neighbors a million dollars, which they shared with Jack, and which he soon wasted buying a flower that was supposed to attract bees made of gold.

Leader: The End. Good job, group. Excellent work turning your imaginations into a fun, creative story.

Variation:

• Hand all the cards to one teller, and let him tell a story using each card in turn.

#94: Distract-a-Story

Game Objective: To keep telling your story no matter what happens
Learning Objective: To enhance our skill of reading the audience
Recommended Ages: 12 to 112
Number of Players: 3 to 30
Energy Level: Medium
Formation: Standing in a circle with the leader in the center
Props: A small, lightweight scarf

Description:

- Explain to your group that, on your mark, they will all begin telling at the same time any story they wish.
- Let them know you will be tossing a scarf in the air and catching it. If the scarf hits the floor, they all need to stop telling at the instant the scarf and the floor meet.
- Any teller who continues telling after the scarf hits the floor will receive a penalty. Each penalty is another distraction added.
- For Round Two, players continue telling their tale, but the teller or tellers who kept talking in the first round must now tell with their left hand over their left eye.
- Continue to play further rounds, adding the following penalties:
  - ✓ While keeping the left hand over the left eye, the right hand now gently taps on the teller's head.
  - ✓ With the left hand over the left eye and the right hand gently patting, the teller needs to slowly spin in place.
  - ✓ With both hands busy and the teller slowly spinning, the teller must continue his story in a loud, monotone.

Variation:

- You may wish to play with everyone adding a distraction each round.

Leadership Tip:

- Use your own creativity to invent your own distractions.

#95: Invention Stories

Game Objective: To entertain the group with an improvised tale

Learning Objective: To use imagination and creation to invent a story about an item's invention

Recommended Ages: 12 to 112

Number of Players: 2 to 12

Energy Level: Low

Formation: Sitting in chairs in a circle

Props: A small bag concealing one dozen or so household items (such as, a cork, a candle, a matchstick, a key, a fork, a spoon, a disposable lighter, a spatula, a pocket knife, etc.)

Description:

- Move around the circle, allowing each player to reach in the bag without looking and pull out an item.
- Give the group about four or five minutes to imagine and create a story about how their chosen item was invented. Each tale should include the name of the inventor and detail about the item's creation.
- Once everyone is ready, go around the circle and share what will be some very interesting tales.
- Example: *Candle*

    "A long time ago, there lived a man named J.J. Waxman. He loved to eat wax. He was frequently stung as a child while stealing bee's wax. Yet nothing could stop J.J. from his love of wax. People used to make fun of J.J. because the front of his shirts were always covered with the wax he'd been eating. It was a messy, messy snack. Tired of being teased, J.J. searched for a way to make his beloved wax less messy to eat. One day, in a butcher's window, J.J. saw the answer in a long string of sausages. With the use of a simple string, J.J. turned his messy snack into a neat, easy-to-eat treat, and if you every visited J.J.'s house, you would find every square inch covered with long sticks of wax with a handy string right down the center. J.J. was very happy until that fateful night when his house caught fire, and J.J. watched as his house, slowly, slowly, *slowly* burned to the ground. The very next day, J.J. patented his million-dollar idea for "J.J. Waxman's Slow Burning Light Stick," which a clever marketing man named K.K. Candle rebranded, making all involved very, very rich."

Leadership Tip:

- Be careful with time. Let folks know their tale should only be around three minutes in length.

#96: Pocket Stories

Game Objective: To entertain the group with your imagination

Learning Objective: To improve basic skills while testing the skills of imagination and creation

Recommended Ages: 15 to 115

Number of Players: 2 to 20

Energy Level: Low

Formation: Sitting in chairs in a circle

Props: What participants agree to share from their pockets

Description:

- Begin by asking the group to remove from one of their pockets or purses an interesting item that they would not mind someone else holding for a short while.
- Ask the participants to hand their item (keychain, coin, picture, nail clippers, etc.) to the person on their right.
- Allow the group about four or five minutes to create a story explaining why the item they are holding is the most valuable item in the entire world.
- Invite participants to share their tales with the group.

Leadership Tips:

- If your group is large, you may wish to limit stories to three minutes in length.
- Being firm about the time limit will help the flow of the game.
- It is a good idea to have a few spare items on hand for the rare person who carries nothing in his pockets.

#97: Worst Homework Assignment Ever

Game Objective: To tell a true tale and a fictional tale so other players can't tell which is which

Learning Objective: To discover forgotten stories

Recommended Ages: 12 to 112

Number of Players: 2 to 24

Energy Level: Low

Formation: Sitting in chairs in a circle

Props: None

Description:

- Invite players to think back over their school years and try to recall their worst homework assignment. It may have been difficult, time-consuming, hard to build, lost, broken, involved others who couldn't get along, taken over by a "helpful" parent, or used an uncooperative pet.
- Once most players have a story in mind, ask them to mentally create a second, entirely fictional tale about a different homework disaster.
- Ask for volunteers who are ready to tell both tales. Ask the group vote on which was the teller's true Worst Homework Assignment Ever.

Leadership Tip:

- You may wish to finish the game by exploring with the tellers if there are any other interesting stories they thought of while recalling their true tale.

#98: Principal's Office

Game Objective: To find the two fibbers in the group
Learning Objective: To discover personal stories players may have forgotten
Recommended Ages: 12 to 112
Number of Players: 4 to 24
Energy Level: Low
Formation: Sitting in chairs in a circle
Props: None

Description:

- Stand in the middle of the circle, and ask the group to firmly close their eyes and stick their left hands into the center. Point out to the group that very few people escape their many years of school without being sent to the principal's office at least once.

- With left hands still held out and eyes closed, ask the participants to raise their right hands if they have ever been sent to the principal's office. Explain that you are going to silently tap two different hands and that those two people should not let on that their hands have been tapped.

- Carefully study your group. Secretly and quietly tap the left hand of a person who has their right hand raised for going to the principal's office, then silently tap the hand of a person who has never been to the principal's office.

- Invite the group to open their eyes. Explain they are all going to either share about the time they were sent to the principal's office or talk about how they are so good they never were sent to the principal's office.

- Just before hearing the first tale, explain the significance of tapping the two hands:
  ✓ Tell everyone that one member of the group who was definitely sent to the principal's office is going to try to convince the group that he was such a good student he never got in trouble, and one other participant who actually never got sent to the principal's office is going to tell a huge fib about a time he got in incredible trouble, ending up in a visit to the principal.

- Have the group share their stories, and then vote to discover who the group thought the two fibbers were.

Leadership Tips:

- There is a small possibility you may not have anyone in one of the categories. In this case, just tap the one hand.

- Some players may wish to take the tack that they weren't that well-behaved, they just never got caught, and that is a perfectly acceptable. Simply encourage them to tell of something they did that should have sent them to the principal's office.

- When the game is over you may wish to spend some time asking if anyone recalled any trouble at school that might make a good story.

#99: Police Stories

Game Objective: To win the vote for best job getting inside a policeman's head
Learning Objective: To discover lost stories and see them from another's point of view
Recommended Ages: 18 to 118
Number of Players: 2 to 20
Energy Level: Low
Formation: Sitting in chairs in a circle
Props: None

Description:

- Explain to the group that rarely does somebody make it through life without one unpleasant or unexpected encounter with a police officer. Give kudos to any in your group to any who have only had pleasant and planned encounters with police.
- Let your group know that they each are going to tell the story of one of their encounters with the police, but they are going to do so in a very different way. Everyone is going to tell their tale in first person, from the officer's point of view.
- Have everyone share their tales, and then vote who did the best job getting into the mind of the police officer they met.

Leadership Tips:

- You may wish to have some other, more silly voting categories such as, The Police Officer Who Should Not Have Got of Bed That Morning, The Meanest/Nicest Police Officer Ever, or The World's Most Patient Officer.
- Some folks may not wish to tell of any encounter they ever had with the police. It is fine for any who wishes to take a pass in this game.
- Depending on your group, it may be better to take volunteers to tell rather than going around the circle.
- Lastly, you may want to reinforce the idea that it is usually the points in life where trouble occurred that stories are hiding.

#100: Pet Tales

Game Objective: To share one true story and one story that *could* be true
Learning Objective: To discover lost personal stories and test imaginations
Recommended Ages: 14 to 114
Number of Players: 2 to 20
Energy Level: Low
Formation: Sitting in chairs in a circle
Props: None

Description:

- Explain to your group that it is human nature to love their pets and tell stories about their pets. Unfortunately, pet stories, by nature, almost always have a sad ending, since humans generally outlive their pets. An audience member will wonder and ask, "Whatever happened to that dog?" "Do you still have that cat?" or "Where's that raccoon now?"
- Let your group know that today you, as a group, are going to fix the fatal flaw of pet stories. Anyone in the group who desires is going to tell two stories: The first is some adventure they had with one of their beloved pets, and the second tale is what the pet is now doing in that pet's Pet Heaven. (Most will find it fun to get inside their pet's head.)

Leadership Tip:

- You will find very few people who haven't owned at least one pet or became friends with a relative's or neighbor's pet. Encourage anyone who says he doesn't have a pet story to invent one about a pet he wishes he had.

#101: Jack Flip

Game Objective: To keep a group story moving when a player does not know when he is telling next

Learning Objective: To reinforce basic in front of an audience skills while exercising the skills of imagination and creation

Recommended Ages: 12 to 112

Number of Players: 4 to 24

Energy Level: Low

Formation: Sitting in groups of four around tables or small circles in chairs or on the floor

Props: One deck of cards per group of four

Description:

- Begin by giving each group a deck of standard playing cards.
- Ask for one person in each group to both hold the cards face down and to be the first card flipper.
- Let your groups know that, on your signal, the person on the right of the card flipper will begin telling an impromptu story about anything he wishes. While he is telling, the card flipper will slowly begin revealing/flipping individual cards from the top of the deck and placing them back on the bottom.
- Explain to the groups that when "Jack" (any of the four) appears, the person on the teller's right will continue the story, and the person who was just telling becomes the new card flipper.
- After every person has gone at least once, let your groups know how much time they have left to finish their tale.

Variation:

- This game can be played in a larger circle with one deck of cards, one card flipper, and one teller at a time for the entire group.

Leadership Tip:

- As always, do what is best for your time and your group. Teams of three, five, and six people also work well.

Appendix A: Games That Best Teach the Essential Skills

The 10 Skills Needed to Perform in Front of an Audience

Facial Expressions

- #44: Family Portrait
- #45: Five-Snapshot Story
- #46: Old Witch Died
- #63: What Would Your Face Look Like If … ?
- #66: Yes, Let's!

Gestures

- #43: Story Statue
- #49: In the Style of Your Adverb
- #54: Textures
- #55: What Are You Doing?
- #61: I Know a Word That Rhymes With …

Eye Contact

- #45: Five-Snapshot Story
- #47: Alphabet Challenge
- #51: Eye Contact
- #52: Applause Meter
- #64: Cover Story

Reading the Audience and Negotiating With the Audience

- #3: By Just Looking at Me
- #19: Word Association Challenge
- #47: Alphabet Challenge
- #52: Applause Meter
- #94: Distract-a-Story

Descriptive Ability

- #59: Describe and Draw
- #68: Rainbow Round Robin
- #76: Last Name Etymology
- #89: Neckties
- #93: Draw and Tell

Tempo

- #11: The Doctor's Dog
- #53: Just a Minute
- #70: Jet Speed Autobiography
- #71: Fast Change
- #87: Number Six Wins

Voice Inflection

- #42: Ka-Blam Name Game
- #58: Who Is That Knocking at My Door?
- #62: Triple Statement Lie Detector
- #64: Cover Story
- #90: Fortunately/Unfortunately

Diction

- #58: Who Is That Knocking at My Door?
- #59: Describe and Draw
- #67: One Word at a Time Story
- #69: Stop Letter Round Robin
- #92: Word to Sentence to Story

Projection

- #42: Ka-Blam Name Game
- #46: Old Witch Died
- #66: Yes, Let's!
- #86: Boiler Burst
- #94: Distract-a-Story

Enthusiasm

- #54: Textures
- #55: What Are You Doing?
- #56: This Is Not A …
- #57: Hitchhiker
- #60: Rock, Paper, Scissors, Cheerleader

The 10 Skills Needed *Before* Performing in Front of an Audience

Imagination

- #54: Textures
- #76: Last Name Etymology
- #84: From the Villain's Point of View
- #90: Fortunately/Unfortunately
- #95: Invention Stories

Discovering Personal Stories

- #4: Most Interesting Place These Shoes Have Been
- #13: Roll and Remember
- #14: Soccer Ball Story Ball
- #91: Scars, Piercings, and Tattoos
- #97: Worst Homework Assignment Ever

Discovering Stories to Make Your Own

- #16: Dear Advice Lady
- #21: Proverb Remix
- #22: Jack Codes
- #81: Story Jumble
- #84: From the Villain's Point of View

Sensory Addition

- #8: "I Have Never …" Chair Swap—Story Prompts
- #13: Roll and Remember
- #54: Textures
- #63: What Would Your Face Look Like If … ?
- #89: Neckties

Word Selection

- #1: Astounding Adjective Name Game
- #11: The Doctor's Dog
- #19: Word Association Challenge
- #20: Word Convergence
- #67: One Word at a Time Story

Powers of Observation

- #9: Observation Challenge
- #10: Pick Three
- #12: Who's Missing?
- #27: Keyboard Olympics I
- #43: Story Statue

Creation and Creativity

- #68: Rainbow Round Robin
- #74: Silly Sentence
- #76: Last Name Etymology
- #77: Someone Famous
- #96: Pocket Stories

Dedication to Practice

- All of the Games!

An Above-Average Understanding and Command of the English Language (or the language in which you are telling)

- #2: Adjective Versus Adverb
- #19: Word Association Challenge
- #26: Two-Brain "Twords" (aka Portmanteaux)
- #32: Whiteboard Olympics I
- #41: Whiteboard Olympics X

An Above-Average Understanding of What Constitutes a "Story"

- #45: Five-Snapshot Story
- #64: Cover Story
- #78: Three Stories, One True
- #84: From the Villain's Point of View
- #93: Draw and Tell

Appendix B:
High- and Medium-Energy Games

High-Energy Games

- #8: "I Have Never …" Chair Swap—Story Prompts
- #46: Old Witch Died
- #54: Textures
- #60: Rock, Paper, Scissors, Cheerleader
- #65: Jungle Tales
- #66: Yes, Let's!
- #86: Boiler Burst

Medium-Energy Games

- #2: Adjective Versus Adverb
- #7: Story Starter Marathon
- #11: The Doctor's Dog
- #12: Who's Missing?
- #14: Soccer Ball Story Ball
- #43: Story Statue
- #44: Family Portrait
- #45: Five-Snapshot Story
- #48: Adverb Challenge
- #49: In the Style of Your Adverb
- #52: Applause Meter
- #55: What Are You Doing?
- #56: This Is Not A …
- #57: Hitchhiker
- #59: Describe and Draw
- #61: I Know a Word That Rhymes With …
- #64: Cover Story
- #70: Jet Speed Autobiography
- #80: Story Balloon
- #81: Story Jumble
- #82: Story Toss
- #85: Firing Squad Story
- #87: Number Six Wins
- #88: Roy G. Biv
- #94: Distract-a-Story

Appendix C:
The Games in Alphabetical Order

Name	#	Name	#
26-Sentence Story	#73	Jack Flip	#101
Adjective Versus Adverb	#2	Jack's Alive	#72
Adverb Challenge	#48	Jet Speed Autobiography	#70
Alphabet Challenge	#47	Jungle Tales	#65
Applause Meter	#52	Just a Minute	#53
Astounding Adjective Name Game	#1	Just Like	#15
Boiler Burst	#86	Ka-Blam Name Game	#42
By Just Looking at Me	#3	Keyboard Olympics I	#27
Cover Story	#64	Keyboard Olympics II	#28
Dear Advice Lady	#16	Keyboard Olympics III	#29
Describe and Draw	#59	Keyboard Olympics IV	#30
Did You Take the Cookie?	#5	Keyboard Olympics V	#31
Distract-a-Story	#94	Last Name Etymology	#76
Draw and Tell	#93	Most Interesting Place These Shoes Have Been	#4
E Is Overused	#17	Neckties	#89
Eye Contact	#51	Number Six Wins	#87
Family Portrait	#44	Observation Challenge	#9
Fast Change	#71	Old Witch Died	#46
Firing Squad Story	#85	One Word at a Time Story	#67
Five Snapshot Story	#45	Pet Tales	#100
Fortunately/Unfortunately	#90	Pick Three	#10
From the Villain's Point of View	#84	Pocket Stories	#96
Hitchhiker	#57	Police Stories	#99
I Don't Like the Consonant …	#50	Principal's Office	#98
"I Have Never …" Chair Swap—Story Prompts	#8	Proverb Remix	#21
I Know a Word That Rhymes With …	#61	Rainbow Round Robin	#68
In the Style of Your Adverb	#49	Rock, Paper, Scissors, Cheerleader	#60
Invention Stories	#95	Roll and Remember	#13
Jack Codes	#22	Roll Play	#75
		Roy G. Biv	#88

About the Authors

Anthony Burcher is an award-winning professional storyteller and "champion liar." His personal stories have humored audiences from coast to coast. His use of recreation in storytelling workshops brings out the story and abilities in the participants. He also teaches for the Jamestown-Yorktown Foundation and has directed summer camp programs, particularly drama camps. He has written and directed more than 12 Christian youth musicals.

Michelle "Mike" Burcher has directed Presbyterian camps for over 25 years. As a Presbyterian minister, she uses storytelling skills in preaching, and especially in telling Bible stories and personal stories around the campfire. She has also served as a small church pastor and campus minister.

Together, Anthony and Mike bring more than 50 years of experience in storytelling and recreation leadership. They co-authored *Making Fun Out of Nothing at All: 101 Great Games that Need No Props*, now in its second edition, and continue to teach the value of joy and play. Married for over 30 years, they have two grown children and care for a menagerie of critters.